The Proposal Writer's Workshop

The Proposal Writer's Workshop

A Guide to Help You Write Winning Proposals

by **VC League**

Copyright © 1998 by VC League

All rights reserved. No part of this book may be reproduced or transmitted in any form or by any means, electronic or mechanical, including photocopying, recording, or by any information storage and retrieval system, without permission in writing from the publisher.

Curry-Co Publications
P.O. Box 231097
Sacramento, California 95823-1097
Fax 916/395-1133

Curry-Co books are available at special discounts for bulk purchases for sales promotions, premiums, fund-raising, or educational use. For details write to above address.

Editor: Odessa Bethea

Designed by: Virginia A. Lathan

Cover Design by: Dora Lee

Printed in the United States of America

Library of Congress Catalog No. 98-93880

ISBN 0-9636195-5-1

To Thelma

Acknowledgment

There are many people who helped me with this book, and I am greatly appreciative of each of their efforts. However, there are a few who I want to give a special thanks to. Asucion Suren and Evelyn LaRue, their encouragement and support was invaluable. Virginia Lathan for her significant technical contribution. And last but not least, Odessa Bethea, my editor, for using her ability and confidence to make *some really tough calls!*

CONTENTS

First Thoughts..*xi*

Author's Preview..*xiii*

✱ ✱ ✱

Changing Times..*1*

    Not-for-profit happenings

The Seven Laws of Money Revisited...............*11*

    A philosophy about money

How to Say It!..*21*

    Important considerations
    for a well written proposal

Program Planning...*45*

    What are you going to do?
    Why are you going to do it?
    And how much will it cost?

Who Are These People?.................**101**

    The importance of credibility

Just Where is the Money?.......................**109**

    Resources to help locate funders

Stalking the Elusive Dollars...................**132**
   in Cyberspace

    The Internet and other on-line resources

"Da Board"..**151**

    Boards of directors' role in fund solicitation

Now What?...**167**

    Some final advice

VC's Recommended Resources..................**172**

    Additional resource information

About the Author....................................**191**

References..**192**

Index..**197**

✳ ✳ ✳

Publisher's Page..

First Thoughts

"**In** the modern industrial world, the principal struggle for survival takes the form of the struggle for money. Money plays an important role when it comes to furthering one's success. A well-managed business offering a superior product or service may still be overwhelmed by a less efficient competitor who is better capitalized. A ballet, play, or movie of great artistic importance will never be produced if its creators cannot attract the necessary funding. Anyone who wishes to accomplish their [sic] goals or claim a share of the earth's abundance must first be prepared to do battle for money."

I read those words in ***Thick Face, Black Heart*** by Chin-Ning Chu and thought she could have substituted the word "organization" for "business" or added "not-for-profit." However, after reading the statement several times, I decided that business referred to all types of organizations, making the statement applicable to the many organizations I work with. Indeed, this idea must be accepted and acted upon if an organization is to survive. If a group, even a successful one, does not generate resources--particularly money--it dies.

Organizations go out of business every day. I have been part of groups so traumatized, and some of them even owned glowing testimonials to their effectiveness. An organization must continually carry out its mission; meet its objectives; and also regularly plan, revise, and update fund development projects so that the synergy developed from all their hard work can create growth.

Chin-Ning Chu goes on to say, "It is never an easy path. If you don't have a worthy idea and superb execution, the money alone cannot save you. It can only prolong the time before you lose it all. So the game of monetary success is not only about getting the money; it is also about having a great idea and being able to keep the money multiplying through worthy efforts."

Throughout *The Proposal Writer's Workshop: A Guide to Help You Write Winning Proposals*, you will be introduced to many strategies, techniques, and skills that will all serve you in furthering the aim of multiplying money through worthy efforts.

Author's Preview

In 1975, while attending my first formal training session on grantsmanship, and before I had enough knowledge and ability, I decided to write a book about program planning and proposal writing. Since that time, for more than 25 years, I have conducted training programs and seminars; consulted with not-for-profit groups, government and educational agencies, and venture capitalists. I served on The Grantsmanship Center's board of directors for nine years, where for five years during the late 1970s and early 1980s I was chair. Since 1990, I have been a trainer for The Center. In 1988, I formed my own training and consulting firm, Vincente` & Associates, through which I assist organizations, plan programs, develop projects, and write proposals for organizations, including those on whose boards I serve.

During the early 1970s when I was a community organizer writing grants in order to get programming money and operating expenses for small, under-funded not-for-profits, I developed a passion for writing. Fortunately for me, the communities where I was working needed resources, and knowledgeable personnel was scarce, so my inexperienced passion and commitment to their programming efforts was most welcomed.

About the same time, I became interested in the workings of systems and organizations, and because I had more interest than skill, I sought mentors. I made connections with knowledgeable, clear-thinking proposal writers and program planners and developers as well as with individuals who understood organizational development. These people began to teach me to write good, solid program planning statements. As a result of developing this ability, and using it, eventually it brought me steady income (not to be confused with financial or job security).

Dr. Edna Martin of Eastside Christian Center (now the Edna Martin Christian Center) in Indianapolis was the first mentor I adopted. She made me aware of the important connection between program planning and fund development. For philosophical reasons more than anything, Dr. Martin was opposed to accepting government money for her organization and programs. Her unwillingness to do so, has left an indelible impression on me. To this day, that impression causes me to routinely explore more than one option when seeking available funding for a project or program. Some of my other mentors who have come after Dr. Martin are Dee Preston, Jack Quinn, Mickey Finn, Dick Keys, Richard Booze, Myles Dougherty, Bailey Jackson, Ed Sanchez, Norton Kiritz, Eve Berry, Lana Hostetler, and Al Orsello. They have taught me countless valuable lessons about my profession. They have helped the neophyte with a dream to become the practitioner who teaches. In *The Proposal Writer's Workshop*, I take the opportunity to share what I have learned--which is an outgrowth of that dream, those experiences, and the guidance of those people. I began writing this book about three years ago, and when I started researching the subject, I discovered many books covering the same information--planning, writing, and funding sources. A few were excellent; most were mediocre. But none had what I deem to be anything different, innovative, or insightful. An overview of *all* the factors--including how to get funds--that contribute to producing successful proposals was missing. This discovery, and a little encouragement from my friends, helped me decide that now was the time for my book on proposal writing. The information included in *The Proposal Writer's Workshop* is given to acquaint readers with using creative program planning and proposal writing and to give them an understanding of organizational issues that may hinder these efforts. All the examples herein are from my experience with individuals and organizations nationwide, representing a variety of communities, programs, economic levels, and racial and ethnic groups. A major part of my work has been directed at substance abuse prevention and related disciplines, but my professional experience with public and private sources covers being involved in a broad spectrum of grant requests. This includes providing assistance to museums, art groups, educational and cultural concerns, social development groups, etc.

Those who have trained with me know that I give participants only practical, usable information. When I conduct a training session--no matter what the subject--I request participation in a process I adapted from one introduced to me by Dr. Bailey Jackson of the University of Massachusetts. I call it: **WHAT, SO WHAT, NOW WHAT.** It is designed to help in analyzing data and determining what to do with it. You can use it while reading this book by stopping at the end of each section and asking yourself these questions:

- *WHAT* is the significance of the information for you or your organization? Does it validate or reinforce something that is going to be done?
- *SO WHAT?* Is anything that has been said important enough to consider doing? Is there new data, or something that gives a new perspective? Can it be ignored? From what you've just learned, is your organization ready to move on?
- *NOW WHAT?* is the important question. What can be done with this information? Can your organization do something different? Can the staff do something differently? What actions will be taken? This may be anything from developing a plan for going online, to enrolling in a technical writing course at a community college.

I make a point of being available for those I train and for those with whom I consult. Your reading my book qualifies you as a participant in my training, so I will now be available to answer questions for you about your career and work in the area of program planning and proposal writing. (See About the Author)

Changing Times

American attitudes are changing toward technology and social issues like education, welfare, and affirmative action. Change is constant whether it is the minor inconvenience of a traffic detour or the life-shattering disruption of a 7.9 earthquake. A successful organization thrives on change and survives it by continually confronting and incorporating it into its structure.

Tom Peters is a well-known business consultant who co-authored with Robert H. Waterman, Jr., the national best seller *In Search of Excellence*. In *The Tom Peters Seminar: Crazy Times Call for Crazy Organizations,* he writes, "Change. Change. Change. We must learn to deal with it, thrive on it....But, we must move beyond change.... Substitute 'abandonment' or 'revolution' instead."

According to my dictionary, "abandonment" means to give up something completely, and "revolution" means to change radically. Peters' writings coincide with my thoughts on program planning: In order to develop successful fund development processes, not-for-profit organizations need to abandon misinformation and radically change the old myths that shape their ideas about program planning. Many people with whom I have provided consultation to or have taught in seminars need to abandon outdated methods and programs that have as much chance of working as most of us have of winning Olympic gold. Ideally, such abandonment and revolution should occur before a forced change comes about because old ideas and strategies have not worked and the organization is on the verge of closing its doors.

Joel Arthur Barker, management consultant and author, wrote about change unique to business and called that change a "paradigm shift." In his book *Future Edge* he wrote, "A paradigm shift is a change to a new game, a new set of rules." Peters' ideas on change and Barker's ideas on paradigms have changed how I approach those to whom I provide direction. I now *insist* that useless rituals be abandoned and replaced with practices that do not waste time, effort, or resources.

Reading about change in this book could inspire you to pursue success by seeking additional funding, incorporating more program planning in your organization, or changing your approach to proposal writing. "Success," as used here, is the ability to make changes that can make a sought after difference with a target group. That difference is manifested by the accomplishment of one's desired outcomes. Additional funding, then, is only one catalyst that can contribute to success.

An organization seeking funds may adjust some operational procedures to ensure a good outcome. Therefore, seeking funding from private or public sources effects changes that take place in not-for-profit (NFP) organizations and in social and cultural programs. Trends also can dictate organizational changes. Below are some trends that affect not-for-profits and are expected to prevail into the twenty-first century:

- More competition for fewer public and private dollars--due, partly, to far less government money being available;
- Funding sources starting to emphasize more and more evaluation and stress outcomes and performance;
- Funding sources that receive increasingly sophisticated requests from a wider variety of groups;
- Funding sources--particularly private--that scrutinize not-for-profits for organizational stability, leadership effectiveness, management skill, and financial health;
- A greater number of organizations merging or collaborating;
- More organizations that provide direct services rather than political or advocacy services;

- More requests from groups to private sources for capital campaigns to provide funding for management development, technological and computer training, or even land acquisition;
- Fewer multi-year grant awards;

Not-for-Profits Are Under Attack

The productive majority of the 1.1 million public service organizations in the United States are increasingly lumped with the nonproductive and abusive minority. Over time, Congress has chipped away at their once routinely given tax-exemptions, and the media has tarnished their images by labeling them "special interest." The future surely holds changes for not-for-profits.

Activities of the 104th and 105th Congresses have also changed the status of not-for-profit organizations over the last few years. The Senate questioned the integrity of the American Association of Retired Persons (AARP) and their stated goal of enriching the experience of aging. Additionally, the 104th Congress proposed to eliminate advocacy and nontraditional charities from the Combined Federal Campaign, the workplace charity program for federal employees. The Senate also introduced a provision that would deny tax-exemption to any 501(c)(3) educational organization that spent money on non-classroom, public educational activities, such as seminars and training programs.

U.S. House Representatives Ernest J. Istook (R-Oklahoma), David M. McIntosh (R-Indiana), and Robert L. Ehrlich (R-Maryland) introduced the Istook Amendment. It was defeated, but had it passed, it would have restricted the amount of federal support to any organization that gives more than five percent of its non-federal expenditures to political advocacy--*not lobbying*, but *advocacy*. Advocacy is a protected right under the First Amendment (to speak publicly in favor of something), yet the obvious intent of the amendment was to keep federally funded organizations from actively and publicly supporting their causes. Imagine the devastating effect such legislation would have had on agencies advocating for the poor or the arts.

The legal system within the American democracy is an adversarial paradigm driven by advocates. To say that a group cannot advocate for or against something is to deny participation in the democratic process. It has been pointed out to me that no one is saying an organization cannot politically advocate for its cause; it just cannot do so while receiving federal funds. But what about community action agencies and organizations that serve the poor and disadvantaged? Most of their funds, if not all, come from public sources. Are these agencies and their clients to be denied their democratic rights? Stay alert; this idea will come before Congress again.

The battle is not only being fought on the federal level, but also on the state and local levels. As local jurisdictions seek to expand financial coffers, they will seek new income sources because no elected official wants to ask constituents for a tax increase. In some cities, we will see jaywalking fines as a source of revenue. In other cities, there will be more parking meters that only accept quarters.

In 1996, in the state of Colorado, a vote for Amendment 11 was placed on the ballot. The main intent of this amendment was to levy property taxes on churches and most other not-for-profits. A coalition of nearly 4,000 private citizens and organizations, organized by the Colorado Association of Nonprofits, worked to defeat it resoundingly. Ann Mitchell Sackey, executive director of the National Council for Nonprofit Associations, in a recent edition of the magazine *Board Members*, warned of the trend toward Amendment 11 copycats in other states. A similar measure has already arisen in the State of Maine, where a state commission proposed that cities be allowed to charge fees to NFPs that do not spend the bulk of their funds on the poor.

Not-For-Profit Management Issue

Some people--many who work in the not-for-profit sector--are critical of the NFP management style. These people believe profit making corporations conduct business more professionally and efficiently. I have heard people say not-for-profits should learn from profit-making businesses. At one time I also entertained that belief. However, my thinking has since broadened, and I now know business finesse does not flow from just one direction. In other words, not-for-profits and profit-making concerns can learn from each other.

This idea about the efficiency of profit-making businesses can be linked directly to our American entrepreneurial spirit. Because we live in a capitalistic system, most of us place great value on free enterprise and rugged individualism. Most of us also adhere to the overriding notion that capitalism and the entrepreneurial spirit will solve all problems. A well-intentioned political candidate may tell the public that he/she will make a good governor or legislator because he/she runs a business and meets a payroll. Even if the candidate is a successful businessperson, that fact alone does not mean that he/she understands the workings of a government that is not strapped to a bottom line. What such a candidate does not say is that each month seventy-three hundred businesses fail. Remember Eastern Airlines, People's Express and Pan American? The Chrysler bailout was not that long ago. Walk around any shopping area in America and notice how quickly restaurants and other small businesses open and close.

Not-for-profits, government agencies, and businesses are different from each other. While all need effective management and leadership, their overall mission, purpose, and desired outcome dictate that each must have a different method of operation. It many ways, it can be more intricate managing and leading a not-for-profit than a for-profit organization because it takes more than financial realities to evaluate a NFP's management staff or its success, or to decide whether the organization fulfilled its mission or achieved its anticipated result.

In a profit-making venture, evaluation is often based on the percentage of increased income over the previous quarter or year. If income does not increase, management and the organization are not successful. After a few years of not making a profit, the business will most likely close down and go out of business.

Even though money is just as crucial to the ability of not-for-profits to stay afloat, their objective for existing is not to simply make more money. In a profit-making concern, the desired end is more money. In an NFP, money is the means, and the outcome is change. Even though NFPs should not be money driven, obtaining and managing money must share priority with management issues. If a NFP's financial picture is rosy, it may be the result of a good fund development plan or a prestigious board of directors. That is good provided the organization is effectively managing its resources and making a difference by carrying out its mission and achieving its objectives.

A board member once proudly said to me that her organization had a great previous year. When I asked why, she said they had a surplus of $20,000. She thought that was a good thing. I think good stewardship that incorporates cost consciousness and conscientious resource management is good. Reasons for a $20,000 surplus may range from not knowing how to make budget projections to not serving all of your clients to not meeting your objectives, etc. Sometimes turning a surplus is nothing more than a red flag for inept management.

I know one board that held on to every penny, even when it meant offering fewer services and not meeting the organization's outcomes. This group was not aware that it might be required to return funds from grant awards carried over for more than a year. That is not being a good steward. A good steward manages the organization's resources and monitors its fulfilling its mission and accomplishing its objectives. Not-for-profits exist to create change, to make a difference, and to do things most people consider unprofitable. And it's because these changes and differences are important to society at large that federal, state, and local governmental bodies allow tax-deductible contributions and give tax exemptions to these organizations.

Moving Forward

Not-for-profit organizations could be in for rough times. Recently, some not-for-profits have seemed less than effective in the eyes of the public. A prime example of this is when the former national United Way director was found guilty of misusing funds. Organizations that work with adolescents have seen drug use and social problems increase. These and other less than desirable outcomes are taking place at a time when individual donors and funding sources expect social conditions and accountability to improve, not get worse. They want their money to make a difference.

Some things can be done to give the American public a sense that NFPs are making a difference. The not-for-profit community can work with Congress and local and state legislatures. At a time of declining public and private funding, NFPs need to keep the public informed of the increasing need for services they provide. In this vein, I--of course--make a pitch for increasing emphasis on program planning, proposal writing, and organizational development. If a program plan is developed and its success publicized, then accountability will be demonstrated. Effective planning, development, and presentation of a well-written proposal are major steps in reclaiming the good image of NFPs.

The Seven Laws of Money Revisited

In 1974, I participated in a ten-day training program in Santa Barbara, California, sponsored by the United States Office of Education, conducted by the University of California at Santa Cruz. While there, I attended Peter Abrams' three-hour workshop on proposal writing, and it's there that I was introduced to *The Seven Laws of Money* by Michael Phillips. The book struck a cord with me because it presents a philosophy about money that successful proposal writers, program planners, and program managers must understand. So immediately upon my return to my home city, I headed straight for Kroch and Brentano's bookstore and bought a copy.

Michael Phillips, I learned, *really* knew about money. Not only had he created MasterCard, but he also had been a top executive with a large San Francisco-based bank and was a decision-maker while at a large philanthropic organization.

For many years I recommended Phillip's book to groups and individuals with whom I worked. Then, suddenly, it seemed to have vanished from the shelves of large and small bookstores alike. I continued to search for it, though, until finally a bookstore clerk told me it was out of print. That is when I made the decision to present the laws here. But as fate would have it, the book was to again become an available resource. On New Year's Eve, 1994, I was traveling from Atlanta to Oakland and had a layover at Chicago O'Hare, so I decided to browse the United Airlines concourse bookstore. And there it was. It was smaller and a different color, but it was indeed the same book, my old friend.

Upon seeing the book in print again, I first thought about dropping this chapter from my book. However, I quickly snuffed that thought because the philosophy behind the laws is too important to the solicitation of funds. Good decision! Because even though I browse bookstores regularly, since that sighting at O'Hare I have not seen the book again.

These laws are not absolutes but are good guidelines for people with whom I consult, people who generally have little understanding of how their philosophy about money relates to the grant solicitation process. I will present five of *The Seven Laws of Money* here. Not only will they provide a fundamental understanding of money in our society, but they also support my belief that continual success in securing grant awards involves much more than submitting well-written proposals.

The First Law
Do it!
Money Will Come When You are Doing the Right Thing.

The First Law is the hardest to accept and is the source of the most distress. It translates to: Go ahead, do what you want to do! Be concerned about your competence and skill, but do not worry about the money.

Half dozen times a year, I attend meetings and watch groups begin to organize around a problem or an identified community need. I listen as their discussion quickly turns to the topic of money: how to raise it and how to use it. This usually brings the organizing process to a standstill before they have even finished outlining a plan.

My advice is this: Do not talk about money the first few meetings; not the cost for hiring staff, renting facilities, or any other thing. Do not let money minutiae make your group neglect the community need or societal pressure that brought everyone together. Designate a committee or individual to identify funding sources and learn fundraising techniques. This person, or committee, can hold separate financial meetings and even participate in regular meetings with the whole group. However, money must not be discussed until a later, more appropriate time.

The essential element of a newly forming organization is a good idea that people want or need, into which they can invest personal energy and time. Making the idea a reality is the reward. Money makes it possible to act on the idea. The First Law tells us to work hard and develop a worthy idea, then the money to carry out that idea will come. In other words, it's the *actual working* on the idea that attracts the money.

The Second Law
Money Has Its Own Rules:
Records, Budgets, Saving, Borrowing

In this law Michael Phillips tells us, "The rules of money are probably Ben Franklin-type rules: never squander it; do not be a spendthrift; be very careful; you have to account for what you are doing; you must keep track of it; you can never ignore what happens to money."

Accountants are the high priests of money and practice the rituals of finance religiously, he tells us. They handle the financial books of a large conglomerate in the same manner as those of a small community-based youth program. As far as managing the finances of the two, the only difference is conglomerates have more money than youth programs, so it takes more time to work through their finances. So what do accountants actually do? They watch incoming resources, record income sources, and keep detailed records of all expenditures. They use income and expense statements, or asset and liability statements, that record in minute detail the categorical flow of money. Accountants make sure someone is responsible for check writing and documenting the origin and destination of funds.

Daily expenses must be tracked; receipts must be kept. Inexperienced people make the mistake of ignoring this essential rule of money handling as do many people who are knowledgeable in money management. The inability to stick to this law is the reason many organizations are unable to gain funding.

The Third Law
Money Is a Dream: A Fantasy as Alluring as the Pied Piper

Money is a state of mind. Phillips maintains that money is a fantasy, purely a dream: "People who go after it as though it were real and tangible, end up...significantly changed in order to reach it. They become quite different from what they set out to be."

Individuals and organizations often have unrealistic expectations of what getting funded will mean to their efforts. Oftentimes, a board member might want to get one big grant so that her group can dispense altogether with fundraising, thereby circumventing the necessary standards that organizations have to adhere to in order to qualify for additional funds. Acquiring such an award is usually a fantasy, and organizations that operate from the mindset of "money solves all" are usually headed for collapse. Money is a communication medium with imaginary value and will not solve every problem or meet the mission of an organization. In the real world, money only records financial transactions. If money becomes the goal, the quality of other objectives is sacrificed.

The Fourth Law
Money Is a Nightmare: Jail, Robbery, Fear of Poverty

Marriages and other relationships end because of the pursuit of money. Families are often destroyed after the death of a wealthy relative because heirs want more money than they were bequeathed. Many people are in jail because they have committed money-related crimes. According to US Department of Justice figures, robbery, burglary, larceny, forgery, auto theft, and drug trafficking make up 70 percent of all crimes. That percentage goes even higher if details hidden under domestic violence are examined. Those who commit these kinds of crimes reach a state where money is wanted so desperately that they are willing to take risks most of us would not. Oftentimes, these people have other options available for overcoming their dilemmas, but they want the quick fix. They're of the mindset that having money is the great cure all, so they mindlessly take the risk, a risk that often leads to all kinds of secondary consequences. Hence, the nightmare begins.

Nonprofit organizations have been destroyed attempting to acquire money. Money can cause staff to bicker, and can also create conflict between directors and boards. For these reasons, the easiest way to disrupt an organization is to give it a large amount of money when it doesn't have the skill to manage it.

Some years ago, I volunteered with a group of men who worked with boys of African descent in the inner-city. We called our organization Babas, which is Swahili for "father." Our program was similar to Big Brothers and Big Sisters, but Babas volunteers also promised to be involved in young people's local events. Evenings, particularly weekends, dressed in our black dashikis and white pants, Babas volunteers roamed the streets talking to youths. Our efforts were so successful that Big Brothers and Big Sisters, Model Cities, and United Way wanted to grant us money. Several other organizations wanted to form collaborative relationships with us. Suddenly we were being pursued. Money was finally coming our way.

But our good fortune turned out to be a Pandora's Box, because within weeks the group was in turmoil. Each of us had become primarily concerned with the number of paid positions, who would get them, and, most important, who would get the director's position. We had to decide where our offices would be, the number of phone lines, who would be in charge of hiring and firing. Our purpose for being a Baba shifted, and Babas ended once money came into the picture.

I am not suggesting we should have remained a volunteer group, but the problem was Babas did not have a formal structure that was ready to receive large sums of money. Many of us were unemployed or underemployed. Once money became part of the equation, we believed jobs might become available. That thinking interfered with the spirit and nature of the group. From that experience, I learned that even though having money is desirous and necessary, organizations must guard against allowing their missions to be disrupted by the pleasures that money can bring. Without a system in place for addressing the changes money brings to an organization, the best of efforts can be corrupted--especially when working with people who are needy, greedy, or in desperate situations.

The Fifth Law
You Can Never Really Give Money Away

In the Fifth Law, Phillips examines money in static and dynamic terms. He describes the relationship created between borrower and lender, seller and buyer, or friend and friend. Over time, he says, money flows in defined channels between these groups and individuals like electricity flows through wires. If money has no flow, it has no value. It is this dynamic flow, not the wires, channels or boundaries that I will focus on here.

If I go to a car rental agency and give the person behind the counter $50, he will let me rent a car for a day. This is an exchange, a two-directional flow. The car rental agency reaps the benefit of receiving the $50, and at the same time, the $50 has enabled me to have transportation. If I give a friend $50 and tell her to use it as she chooses, that it is a gift, there is no requirement for the money to directly flow back to me because it was given freely, with no expectation of a return. However, my ongoing relationship with the person means that money and other things of value can flow between us. For example, if she and I are dining out, she might pick up our dinner tab. In this instance, even though the tab may be more or less than $50, I still will have reaped the benefit of an indirect flow of money.

Under the right circumstances, money can flow between a funder and fund seeker and back to the funder. For instance, let's say a corporation executive makes a derogatory remark about Latino Americans. This puts the Latino community up in arms, and they become quite successful at keeping the incident in the media spotlight. As a result, the corporation's public image is badly tarnished; demand for its products is decreasing. There's a need for damage repair. The corporation's advertising director suggests immediately developing a heart warming TV commercial featuring a Latino family using its products. However, the director of corporate giving has another suggestion. She has received a proposal from a school consisting predominately of Latino American students. The program's objective is to within one year increase its senior students' reading scores by one grade level. The corporation contacts the school expressing its interest in funding the proposal. However, they would like another component added to it. They feel the most successful students (a small number) could be rewarded in another way. Upon graduation, if they desire, they can be hired by the corporation in entry-level positions. This is the making of a win-win-win situation: the corporation has become involved in a good-for-their-image, good-for-their-soul venture; the school gets its program funded and, hopefully, increases the student's reading scores; the students read better and are presented with another avenue of employment upon graduation. In this scenario, the money has flowed quite dynamically.

Summary

Michael Phillips' First Law of Money is best summed up by the ideals of the late Joseph Campbell, professor, author, and demystifyer of myth and legend: "Follow Your bliss and the money will come." When the money comes, the remaining laws tell how to handle it traditionally and wisely. Understand borrowing and budgeting, the purpose of record keeping, and saving, as well as the duties of an accountant. But also understand money only has value as a medium of exchange. It's *how* you determine money should flow and then *allowing* it to do so that gives it its real value.

How to Say it!

Important Considerations for a Well-Written Proposal

Many factors will determine whether your program gets funded. The prime factor is the quality of your proposal, because it may be the only way a funding source can get specifics about your organization and program. Your proposal should be well written and easy to read. Along this line, a few years ago I saw Maya Angelou, poet and author of the bestseller *I Know Why the Caged Bird Sings,* on a local TV talk show in San Francisco. She said something then that I always keep in mind and tell other proposal writers: "Anything that is easy to read is hard to write."

Proposal writing is not easy and should not be done hastily no matter how often you do it. A lot of effort goes into the completion of a well-written proposal, and if you inform you colleagues and work associates of this, they may not only be more supportive of your efforts but may also be more realistic about what you can accomplish through the process. I cannot say how many times I have heard an executive director or board member of an agency say "All she had to do was write a proposal." "That's *all* she had to do?" is usually my response...along with a few other well-chosen, diplomatically couched, comments. As I work with proposal writers around the country, I hear many misconceptions like this about proposal writing.

Some of you may have had this experience. Your executive director comes hurrying into your office waving an envelope and yelling, I just got this RFP (request for proposal), or RFA (request for application), and a proposal must be written by next Tuesday. The bad news is this is Thursday morning and your weekend is flying out the window. The good news (if you can call it that) is this is a three-day weekend, so you have an extra day to develop a plan. By Monday you and a support staff person--if luck prevails--will be in the office working your butts off. Does this sound familiar? It does to me because this scenario falls into my been-there-done-that category, and I do not like it. This occurrence should be an exception, something that happens once every blue moon. Before a solid proposal can be written, you must have a program planned. It is a poor proposal written without knowledge of the program. Program planning is the first step toward a well-written proposal, and you as a proposal writer must have a thorough understanding of the program.

Equally important to producing a well-written proposal is for the actual writer of it to have a grasp on the mechanics of writing--grammar, punctuation, sentence structure, word usage...to name a few. If your writing skills are deficient, you must improve them. There are several ways for doing this. Buy and use a style writing manual and other books on nonfiction writing. I currently use *The New York Public Library Writer's Guide to Style and Usage* as my final reference arbiter. For day-to-day references I use *The Associated Press Style Book and Libel Manual* and *A Writer's Reference* by Diana Hacker. Other good reference books are *The Chicago Manual of Style* and, from first-year college English, *The Elements of Style* by William Strunk, Jr. and E. B. White. To be a serious proposal writer, I tell clients, have at least one style writing manual and one other skill-builder writing book. Add to your library continually.

Keep in mind when preparing to write a proposal that it will represent your organization and what it proposes to do. It is equivalent to making an oral presentation. Picture yourself standing before a distinguished panel of a funding source making a formal presentation. What questions will this panel ask about your organization? What will the panel want to know about the project? Will it want to know why this approach or program was chosen? Yes, of course, it will. Just as any person would attempt to answer these questions as articulately as possible when standing in front of the panel, they should be answered the same in your written presentation-- the written proposal.

Writing the Best Proposal

According to the cliche`, your proposal should be "easy to read and easy to follow" because someone will read it. Do not use footnotes, reference pages, full-page graphs, charts or photographs within the body of the document unless the funding source requests it. It is best to include these type items in an appendix so they don't detract from the proposal narrative. However, keep in mind that the appendix is not a landfill, so do not use if as a dumping ground for extraneous information. Anything included in the appendix should be referred to in the body of the proposal. Even though a proposal is a technical document, many techniques required in academic writing are not always appropriate for it. As much as practical, you should use basic words and terms that a layperson can understand. Obviously, this is a rule of thumb, and if you are responding to a RFP, or other guidelines, that requires technical specificity, then by all means comply.

If your proposal is being submitted to a local, state, or federal agency, most likely it will be reviewed by three to seven readers. If your proposal is submitted to a private agency, the number of readers varies. I sometimes jokingly suggest to clients that they excessively imagine an infinite number of diverse people are going to read their proposals. But when I really think about it, that thought is probably more real than imaginary. For example, I recently read some application material put out by the Office of Community Services, Minnesota Department of Children, Families and Learning. It was to solicit proposals for funding four intervention and prevention program grants. It said:

> "Review teams reflect the diversity of communities. Based on the fund categories, teams may include youth, parents, educators, youth workers, county attorneys, county social services workers, juvenile justice service providers, public health specialists, law enforcement officials, state agency representatives, civic, business and faith community members, and other citizens. Over 400 people volunteered to review 560 applications in 1997."

This makes it crucial to ensure that the proposal is written so that people from diverse backgrounds can easily evaluate it and understand the program plan. A technique I use to keep the importance of addressing this requirement in the forefront of my thoughts when writing proposals is to chant this mantra: "Let all who read understand. Let all who read understand...."

It is not always known to an agency where a proposal it submits will be reviewed. A public funding source may bring reviewers together at a central location so they can read and rate proposals. If the readers come together in the same room at the source's office, the reviewers may be more critical of inaccuracies in your proposal because they are influenced by the collective standards of the review team.

In another situation, to reduce costs, the funder will send copies of proposals to each reader's location. The reader may have a couple of weeks to rate submissions and will not be influenced by others. Nevertheless, other factors come into play. Proposals may be reviewed at any time throughout the day or night, so individual time management becomes an issue. I have experienced this situation, and the distractions can be many. Issues from the reviewer's "real" job or emergencies from his family can tempt one to leave proposal reading to the last minute. So the easier the proposal is to read, the more apt it is to engross the reviewer and command his undivided attention. Or, to put it another way, I quote Strunk and White in *The Elements of Style,* "...the surest way to arouse and hold the attention of the reader is by being specific, definite, and concrete."

The foundation selection process often gives an initial reader the power to decide whether a particular proposal matches the foundation's objectives. The proposal writer's first goal, then, is to know the funder's purpose, and to make sure his proposal fits that purpose. Otherwise, your program will lose its chance for funding without ever making it out the gate.

Thorough proofreading and editing are essential. Make sure your document is proofed and edited by different people. It is surprising how many writers with whom I have worked believe they can write a proposal and also do the final editing. Of course that is not true.

Write at least four drafts. When writing your first draft, do not attempt to edit; just write. This draft will contain every fact and idea--important or not--concerning the proposal being developed. Once the first draft is completed, let several people review it, and ask for comments regarding each section. Analyze this feedback and use it to possibly make changes that will be incorporated into your second draft.

From draft number two, strike all nonessential information and begin to organize information by category. Upon completion of this draft, ask a trustworthy associate to give you some honest, specific comments on how well the program has been outlined and on the way the proposal is written. Use those comments to possibly make additional changes.

Once the third draft is written, give it what I call the "English teacher test." Every writer needs an English teacher. Why? Because the person writing the document may not see things that someone who has not worked on it can see. Whether you are proficient in grammar or not, find a qualified person to be your English teacher. Do not let your self-assurance persuade you differently; a fresh set of eyes must look at the proposal.

Again, after each review, you must seriously consider any recommended changes or corrections, otherwise you defeat the process.

Sometimes you may not have available to you a person who is skillful enough to examine your proposal for its adherence to the rules governing correct word usage and other aspects of writing. However, one possible way to still get this scrutiny is by accessing a grammar hotline. Other than perhaps the cost of a toll call, these grammar hotlines are free of charge. They are staffed by college and university volunteers around the country. In the United States and Canada, 50 such sites exist. Call you local library for information on one near you.

William Lutz writes about language and clarity from another perspective. He is a professor of English at Rutgers University Camden, New Jersey, campus and a member of the Pennsylvania Bar. In his book *The New Doublespeak: Why No One Knows What Anyone's Saying Anymore,* he talks about the connection between signs, symbols and words. Lutz points out that signs have an easy-to-understand, natural connection to what they signify. A one-to-one relationship exists with their meaning. For instance, the meaning of a red octagon with "STOP" emblazoned across the middle is recognized by almost all (if not all) licensed drivers in the United States as a stop sign. Upon seeing it, they know to stop. They may choose not to stop, but that most likely has nothing to do with their knowledge of the meaning of this sign. However, Lutz explains, no obvious or natural connection exists between symbols and what they represent. Their meaning is contrived and arbitrary, strictly for convenience. A word is a symbol. No direct connection exists between a word, what it stands for, or what it means. His research shows that 500 of the most frequently used words in the English language have 14,000 different meanings. "Family" and "values" are two words used a lot together during political campaigns. But just what are family values? Your definition may differ from mine and both of ours may differ from someone else's.

In a proposal, many words are used that symbolize uniformly recognized conditions or circumstances to all those working in the same field. But these symbols are abstractions; they do not mean the same thing to everybody, everywhere. Their ability to project a very specific picture to others in your field of work may get lost when trying to make a point in a proposal submitted to a funder. The funder could be left with a cloudy, ambiguous picture of what your proposal is expressing. To avoid this, make sure your proposal is as universally clear as possible by choosing the simplest words and phrases. Avoid jargon and buzzwords. Minimize the use of overworked, nonspecific adjectives and adverbs like "unique" and "innovative." Almost every proposal I have ever read has included statements such as these: This unique problem.... This innovative program. . . *What* is the unique problem? *Why* is this program innovative? If a word is not fully descriptive, then either don't use the word or make sure you include an explanation of what is meant by it.

Professor Lutz describes "doublespeak" as the conscious use of language as a weapon or tool by those in power to achieve their ends at the expense of others. Unfortunately, proposal writers and other professionals have picked up this technique of using language. By matching the following doublespeak phrases with what is really meant to be said, you can gain a clear understanding of what Lutz means by doublespeak.

Doublespeak
1. Employee repositioning
2. Air curtain incineration
3. Maximum incapacitation
4. Human biodynamics
5. Creating an age-controlled environment

What it Means
A. Tavern
B. Focusing on retirement
C. Physical education
D. Burning garbage in open pits
E. Death

(Answers are at the end of this chapter.)

A doublespeak phrase I often see in proposals is "maximum community participation." Does it mean total community involvement in the proposed effort, or does it mean the recipient organization will communicate with everyone in the target area? I admit that at one time I have used this phrase--and other doublespeak terms--in proposals because I thought they sounded good and made me appear to have reduced a problem, objective, or activity to its least common denominator. And at the time of doing so, I quite possibly did not clarify what my exact meaning was. But what is important is that in my efforts to refine my writing, I am ever watchful for these types of ambiguous terms and work hard at replacing them.

Another word showing up repeatedly in proposals, that I want to call special attention to, is "collaboration." "Because the funding source expects to see it," I am often told. My assessment of this is it is not the *word* collaboration but the *strategy of collaboration* that the funding source wants to see. Proposal writers must pay attention to this distinction.

One of the most powerful influences on our choice of words and how we express ourselves is the media. Because advertisers invent catchy words and phrases to persuade us to buy (often in 60 seconds or less), we are bombarded with nonspecific words that we incorporate in our vocabularies. But when writing proposals, nonspecific expression must be guarded against, and the best ways to do this is by keeping a watchful ear, analyzing our writing, and having someone other than ourselves check our proposals for specificity.

To really underscore the need to communicate more clearly, even the Clinton administration has been announcing its mandate that starting October 1st of 1998 more emphasis will be placed on using plain English when producing federal documents. And to go a step further, by January 1, 1999, federal regulations will also be written in such a way.

Another consideration to keep in mind when writing your proposal is to not "speak down" to your readers by writing in at a sophomoric level. For instance, write about "the satisfaction that comes with a job well done" rather than "how much fun it was when the work stopped." When I recommend using basic, easy-to-understand words, I am by no means suggesting that you write like you are writing for a group of fourth graders. What I am saying is use a combination of words and expressions that convey the true meaning of what you are trying to say, and say it at the level professionals communicate on when talking to each other.

Language and Grammar Guidelines to Watch for When Finalizing a Proposal

1. **Proposal Narrative.** Use the declarative-narrative style of writing in which the facts are stated in chronological and logical order so that the story of your project is clearly revealed. It is the style seen in your daily newspaper.

2. **Subject and Predicate.** Be sure your subject and verb agree with each other: The director requests... Grant recipients require... Check the finished product with your computer's grammar checker. It will not catch everything, but it is helpful.
3. **Sentences.** Use a variety of sentence lengths. A proposal made up of strictly short sentences will be choppy. On the other hand, one composed of strictly long sentences will ramble or be confusing.
4. **Paragraphs.** Confine yourself to one topic per paragraph. This technique makes your proposal easy to read and reference.
5. **Headings and Subheadings.** Using headings and subheadings is a small courtesy to the reader that carries big dividends. A piece of critical information can be easily found.
6. **Pronouns.** Use pronouns clearly: "The staff, along with volunteers, worked hard on getting the proposal funded. They will now work on getting the program in gear." Do not make the reader wonder whether the "they" refers to the staff or the volunteers, or both.
7. **No broad generalizations.** Think of the proposal as a legal document that needs specificity: "Our goal is to cut the number of dropouts by 20 percent in New West High School. We are asking you to contribute $15,000 to help us implement

our plan for doing that."
8. **Conciseness.** Even if your organization's glorious history could be written, no one would want to read that much detail. Know what areas are important to your source, and cover those.

If the mechanics of writing is not your strong point, look up the reference works that I have mentioned in this section. For a nice overview, try Jefferson D. Bates' book *Writing with Precision*. Also, working with an editor and proofreader can be a practical additive for supplementing your own deficient writing ability.

Unsupported Statements and Assumptions

Proposals should not contain any unsupported statements or assumptions. This was first made clear to me more than 20 years ago when I was a participant in a training program at The Grantsmanship Center. Using unsupported assumptions or statements in proposals is the number one mistake proposal writers make. No matter how much education a person has or how many proposals they have written, this remains a pesky issue. In other forms of writing, footnotes and reference pages are included to back up factual statements. Even though these methods are generally not used (or needed) in proposals, it is necessary to cite sources parenthetically in the proposal body.

Broad, general problem or need statements are the most common unsupported assumptions found in proposals: "The Valley community has a drug problem." This may be true, and even evident, but you must tell the potential funder how you've reached this conclusion. It is unwise to assume that a funding source will accept your unsupported statement. Support your statement with excerpts from studies, surveys, or the research of known authorities. Supportive statements can easily be incorporated in your writing by saying such things as "according to...," "as verified by....," "the Mayor's report on this issue further validates...," "(Appendix A)." A technique I use to weed out unsupported statements in proposals I write, and review, is to ask the question: Who says so?

Eliminating unsupported statements is not only necessary in identifying problems, but they must also be eliminated in justifying your objectives or methods. Let us say your organization has established the fact that the community has a drug problem, as documented by a university study and law enforcement records. You also need to familiarize the funder with how this problem is affecting your community: what are the consequences for your target group? Statistics and numbers do not always tell the whole story. Your proposal must answer the funder's question of: So what?

Let's continue. Your organization cares about the drug problem in the community, or this proposal would not have been prepared. But just your organization's caring about a problem is not enough of a justification to be awarded money. Build some support by identifying other credible groups and institutions that are also concerned. In other words, giving concrete examples that show the community as a whole is behind your efforts, answers another crucial question funders ask: Who cares?

"Flag waving" is a time-honored practice in proposal writing: What is good for our community is good for America! Our President says domestic violence must be stopped. The writer is trying to sell the proposal with an emotional appeal. This does not say anything about the *specific actions* that will be taken to eradicate domestic violence in a *specific community*. To keep from making unsupported emotional appeals, answer the question: How will the job get done?

You should use a combination of quotations and endorsements, statistical data or case examples to support your point. Keep in mind, though, when referring to ideas or work that is not your own, the source should be identified. This mainly refers to statements of fact, proven theories, or statistical compilations. General information that is obtainable from various sources can be used without a citation. For example, if you say that New York is one of the five largest cities in the United States, no citation is needed because this is common information verifiable through many sources.

It is not always necessary to obtain permission to use excerpts or quotes. Under copyright law, "fair use" can be made of published materials without seeking permission. This allows use of a few lines from a short article, or a couple of paragraphs from a longer piece, without permission of the publisher. Longer quotations of chapters or sections may require permission. However, including things in a proposal that require a publisher's permission to quote is not something that usually is done..

Nondiscriminatory Language

This riddle has been around a while. There are variations on the theme, but I heard this version most recently. A father took his son out for a drive in his new Viper sports car. Unfortunately a reckless driver swerved in front of their vehicle and caused a head-on collision. Two ambulances arrived at the crash site and took the father to one hospital and, surprisingly, the son to another. After being examined, it was determined that the young man, the son, needed surgery. Later, upon entering the operating room, the surgeon looks down at the patient, steps back gasping and says, "I cannot perform this operation; it's my son!" The question is how could this happen? What is your answer? I will come back to the riddle in a moment.

I think that talking about the use of sexist and other biased language when discussing writing is important, particularly with proposal writing.

This is so because a reader may interpret your use of certain words as the attitude of your organization regarding its clients, supporters, and community.

Let us look at sexist language. I see a lot of it in proposals. I'm not talking about language that shows a genuine contempt for men or women (that is usually not seen in proposals), but rather language that portrays stereotypical thinking that says all secretaries are always women or managers are always men. Sexists thinking assumes that all of one's readers are all men or all women. Let's go back to the riddle. Did you fall victim to the stereotype?

The following sentences, as first phrased, are sexist. Following each is a non-sexist alternative.

A. After a court reporter court reporter graduates, she faces a difficult state board examination.

B. After a court reporter graduates, he or she faces a difficult state board examination.
++++

A. Running for City Council are W.W. Smith, a teacher, and Mrs. D.D. Watson an English professor and mother of three.

B. Running for City Council are W.W. Smith, a teacher, and D.D. Watson, an English professor.
++++

A. If you are a city government official, your wife is required to report any gifts she receives.

B. If you are a city government official, your spouse is required to report any gifts he/she receives.

++++

A recent practice that has sprung up to help avoid using sexist language in general usage writing is substituting the plurals--they, them, their--for the masculine pronouns--he, him, and his--used to refer to persons of either sex. However, those who are sticklers for grammar balk at this and prefer using "her/his, she/he, or him/her." Rewording the sentence to avoid the problem is often the simplest option.

It is not as imperative to be concerned about using a quotation that has sexist language because the sexism is expressed by the *author of the quote*, not you, the *author of the proposal*. However, if you find the quotation as written to be too obtrusive to what you are writing, use a paraphrase rather than the exact wording. You can also freely change words in a quotation, be it to correct sexist language or other errors, as long as you indicate in brackets that you've made a change.

Naming the Population

When working with a group, ask the members of the group what they want to be called. I get a little nervous when I am working with an organization that is not sure how to address a client group, because that indicates to me they may not know their client population as well as they should. What people want to be called varies from community to community. For example, some people of color may want to be called African Americans, or Blacks, or Americans of African descent. Labeling people can be a sensitive issue. The best solution is simple: ask.

Naming your group is not necessarily an issue of political correctness. To many, naming something is power. Haig Bosmajian in his book, ***The Language of Oppression,*** says:

"It isn't strange that those persons who insist on defining themselves, who insist on this elemental privilege of self-naming, self-definition, and self-identity encounter vigorous resistance. Predictably, the resistance usually comes from the oppressor, or would-be oppressor, and is a result of the fact that he or she does not want to relinquish the power which comes from the ability to define others."

Think about it, how would your mom or dad respond to your telling them that you were changing your name. The people I know who have changed their names tell me their parents usually do not call them by the new name. I have had a little experience with this because my mother always called me "Vincente," not "VC."

I have gained awareness and understanding of this issue by working with a variety of communities and people. One of my most poignant memories around this issue is when sometime ago I was working with the Lakota Sioux of South Dakota. As we were writing their proposal, I asked: "Should we use 'Native American' or 'American Indian'?" "We prefer 'Lakota Sioux,'" was the answer. I was completely embarrassed. Rather than allowing them to name themselves, I had presumed they would select one of my two choices.

Public agencies commonly use the term "physically challenged" or "handicapped" for people with disabilities, but the only people I know who call themselves handicapped are bad golfers. I have worked with people who do not like the term "mentally retarded." Yet, those who are familiar with the Special Olympics know that organization uses the term. Easter Seal and other similar organizations maintain a glossary of appropriate names for a variety of groups. If a good working relationship is desired with any group of people, call them what they want to be called. The last thing to do is make assumptions about this based on your own values and beliefs. If an ideal name cannot be found for your target group, and for the sake of writing a proposal you're forced to choose one, choose one that is at least accurate according to common usage, then include an explanation in the proposal about your chosen label. For example, because this target population consists of both Mexican Americans and El Salvadorian immigrants, throughout the writing of this proposal, I have chose to refer to them as "Hispanic."

Also, remember the "*People* First Rule" is widely accepted and may save a lot of headaches. Do not say "W.W. Smith is a diabetic"; say "W.W. Smith is a person with diabetes." The idea is to place emphasis on the person, not on his/her disability or uniqueness.

This subject is important for proposal writers because it may help a reader determine the credibility of your work with a group and whether your agency is the appropriate one to continue that work. The credibility of agencies has been questioned because of the words they chose to refer to their organization or their target group. Again, it will help to know a little about the funding source so you can be guided by their convictions in this matter. This subject is much too complicated to limit to a few paragraphs. Get serious about bias-free writing and get copies of Rosalie Maggio's book, *The Bias Free Word Finder,* and Jean Gaddy Wilson's book, *Working with Words*.

Final Considerations

Your request is more compelling when your proposal is written so that it focuses on the needs of the clients and others who will benefit from the program. Client-driven proposals are not new, but many organizations cannot tell client needs from their own. Nowhere is this more true than in bureaucracies. In the late 1800s, Max Weber, a prominent social scientist in Germany, observed that all bureaucracies tend to allow the means to become the end. They focus on following a process and do not pay enough attention to the results of their actions in trying to adhere to the process. Quite possibly the process they follow may not lead to meeting the needs of their clients, and in many cases it can actually be a hindrance. Even though that statement was made over a century ago, unfortunately, it still holds true today. When a proposal writer writes that his agency needs a new computer, new vehicle, or more staff, they are not asking for money for things that will go directly to their clients. One agency I worked with requested a computer in a proposal so they could move into the twenty-first century. Using this situation, a better way they could have expressed such a request is to have first stated their clients' need to receive information more quickly about jobs that are available in the community. And then saying something like, "We will use the computer to get information to our clients from our state's employment development department within 24 hours of downloading it."

Finally, your proposal should be positive in tone. Even if requesting funds to address a serious problem or need, your document's perspective should be positive. Make it clear that you can make the difference. Convince the funder that the problem is not insurmountable and that your organization has the ability to contribute to solving it. I used the word "contribute" here, because not all problems can be irradiated completely by the efforts of one entity. Sometimes problems are compound and a complete solution to them goes way beyond the capability of one group. In other words, be positive, but also be clear and realistic about what impact you can have on any situation. Don't set yourself, or your agency, up for failure. And remember, an oral emotional appeal can elicit support for your efforts, but when submitting a written document, it will be one of possibly many that a funder has to consider, so don't rely on pure emotion; add substance.

*1-E; 2-D; 3-B; 4-C; 5-A.

Program Planning

**What are you going to do?
Why are you going to do it?
And how much will it cost?**

An essential ingredient to writing a successful proposal is having developed a well-thought-out and well-planned program. Ideally, first develop a program, next identify a compatible funding source, and then write the proposal. Don't focus on a funding source while developing a program, even if one has been identified. Focus on addressing the needs of your target group, your clients, and the other beneficiaries of your effort. For example, if an agency is considering developing a gang prevention program that will target fifth and sixth grade students, the agency's program development and planning should identify not only what the targeted youths will gain from the program, but it should also show how other segments of the community will benefit. How will local merchants benefit? Will any other students benefit? Will the faculty benefit? Will neighborhood parks be safer? What will the community's residents gain from the efforts?

Effective program development should also be outcome driven. Agencies often develop a program driven by a method or strategy. The number one error that program developers make is confusing program objectives with methods. Do not get locked into a particular method or strategy, but stay focused on the expected results. To do this, determine what outcomes are desired based on the identified need. This allows for more flexibility in program development by encouraging the exploration of a variety of methods. If a method that is proposed is too costly, it can be replaced with less-costly options that can achieve the same results.

Program developers and planners who are method-driven rarely consider alternative ways of achieving outcomes. An example I use in trainings to make this point is I tell my participants that my objective is to speak Spanish well enough in twelve months to use it in my work. That is the desired outcome. Now, in choosing the means, or method, to do this, I have several options. One option--and my personal favorite--is to go live in Mexico or Puerto Rico for four or five months and attend a school that teaches Spanish as a second language. Option two, I go to a school in Oakland, California, where I live, that specializes in Spanish as a second language. Let's say the class meets six hours a day for two weeks. With both of these options, I must take into account my work schedule and income generated from working. Can I afford to take off four or five months and go to Mexico or Puerto Rico? Can I afford to take two weeks off to attend classes locally? I have to assess the cost of each of these two options. How much is tuition? How much will it cost to live in Mexico or Puerto Rico? A third option is to attend a local institute on weekends or in the evening, or take a Spanish class at a community college. An option suggested by some of my colleagues who speak

English as a second language is to study from a Spanish textbook and supplement that with listening to Spanish-speaking radio stations and spending time in restaurants, or other places where Spanish is spoken, so I can converse with others.

The point is, there are many methods whereby I can learn to speak Spanish, but in order to make the best selection for my particular need, I have to consider other factors such as cost, time, and practicality. If I truly want to learn to speak Spanish, my focus should be on that outcome, not going to Mexico or Puerto Rico.

A publication that can be especially helpful with program planning and development is The Grantsmanship Center's *Program Planning and Proposal Writing*. Written by Norton J. Kiritz, executive director of The Grantsmanship Center, this classic on the subject has provided program developers and grant writers with detailed assistance for more than two decades. A second book that is also helpful in this area is *Developing Successful Programs*. I, along with two of my colleagues, wrote it as a quick guide to give basic yet essential information to teams of people working at developing programs and writing proposals. Readers have found it particularly helpful in developing and writing program objectives. These two publications are still in print and can greatly help to simplify the task of writing a proposal.

The format proposals takes varies. Oftentimes a RFP greatly influences that, but other times a solicitor merely uses a style of his or her choosing that best presents the needed information.

Because there are so many different proposal formats, I won't take the time here to detail a program planning model or format. I will, however, share a few thoughts on the process.

Gathering Information

Sometimes finding sufficient information about a target population and its geographic area is difficult for program planners and proposal writers, so they plan with inadequate data. At least half of all program planning and proposal writing occurs without the benefit of data from needs assessments. As social problems have become more complex, the importance of good needs assessments has grown.

What is a needs assessment? Simply put, a needs assessment is an activity that attempts to find and categorize information or data on a specific population group. The results of this gathering of information may be used strictly to plan a program or support facts delineated in a proposal, or they may be compiled into a report or other measuring instrument. The term "needs assessment" is also used to refer to the product (the report itself) produced by the information gathering activity.

It is extremely difficult, if not impossible, for a positive, lasting effect to be made on a target population without first understanding their concerns, problems, and needs. You must collect and analyze data about the population group. Do not just crunch numbers gathered from public records or studies, but also become familiar with their attitudes about their environment and issues that affect them. Work at synthesizing how they as a group feel about today's issues, what is important to them, what is their view of the world, how their world view relates to their day-to-day life, what community institutions they hold dearly, which ones they reject. Come up with your own definition or description of their community, but only after you have explored questions like these.

When beginning to develop your needs assessment, pretend you know absolutely nothing about the target group and its geographic area. (Most people I work with do not live in the area they are targeting for their services and are under informed about its location and needs.) Keep *your* values and beliefs out of the picture, particularly your political, economic, religious, cultural, and educational values. To get to this value neutral state, I use what my colleague Ed Sanchez calls the "Freirian Stance," an assessment technique based on the work of Paulo Freire.

The Freirian Stance

In his paper ***Diversity and Prevention***, Sanchez writes the following regarding this approach:

> Paulo Freire had long been recognized for his work in education following his book ***Pedagogy of the Oppressed.*** What he outlined was not only a method of teaching

others and how they would learn, but a process that established a posture for those seeking to provide to others if they were to gain acceptance and participation from the 'client.' To paraphrase his mode, service providers who consider themselves the solution assume the powerlessness of the clients as central to the relationship. In this type of relationship, not only does the client assume the role of oppressed, but the service provider becomes, and may be seen as, the oppressor. Freirian approaches would suggest that the program provider would be ignorant of the client and their situation, thus, the provider assumes a stance as the learner/client and provider and allows the client the same stance. This is a mutual relationship that allows the service provider to collect valuable data needed to understand the client's perceptions of problems and the nature of the client. It also allows a client to participate in the solutions and to cooperate with the program.

Taking a Freirian Stance is useful when conducting a needs assessment, because it facilitates getting information that comes directly from the target group and other key people. For example, a "key informant" most often refers to a titled leader in the community but can also refer to an untitled or informal leader. An informal leader is a person who has influence but may not have a title or official duties. I call a person like this "the mama" or "the teacher." Oftentimes these informal leaders are only found out about if you solicit data directly from a targeted population.

A reliable needs assessment includes "people data" and documented facts. People data is what individuals think, believe, and see. Collect this information from conversations within focus groups, one-on-one interviews, or written questionnaires. Facts come from census reports, police records, court records, or other public sources of information. Having a mixture of both these categories of information in your needs assessment is important whether you're involved with fund solicitation for education, leisure services, arts and cultural pursuits, etc. A good problem statement must be based on a needs assessment that factors in anecdotal information with data collected from official documents.

There are a number of good books on this subject. One in particular is *Needs Assessment: A Manual for Community Action*, which was written by Joanne Guillery and Virginia Lathan. It outlines a step-by-step process based on a needs assessment conducted in a Midwestern community.

Problem Statement

Albert Einstein in essence said that a problem must first be defined before it can be solved. That reasoning is why I consider the problem statement to be the most significant component of successful program planning and proposal writing. Once the problem is thoroughly identified and understood, program planning becomes simpler. Conversely, if the problem statement of a proposal does not adequately define the problem, that can greatly decrease the chances for getting funded. The purpose of the problem statement is to describe the nature and the extent of the problem that has resulted in the need for the proposed program. And, of course, it should also very specifically identify the population that the problem impacts and what part of that population (if not all of it) will be the group targeted for your agency's programming efforts.

Sometimes the words "problem" and "need" are used interchangeably. This is even a practice of many funding sources, and also throughout this book you may notice that. However, in dealing with technicalities, there are distinctions between the two that are worthy of discussion. Data needed to document a problem is different from the data required to substantiate a need. A problem is more accurately defined as a flaw, deficiency, or inadequacy in some system or structure, like the employment opportunity structure in a community, or the dysfunction in a family system. The problem becomes societal when many communities begin to experience it. By this time, there are usually varied statistical reports to substantiate its being labeled a problem. Something characterized as a need usually relates more to a specific population and it focuses on a gap or void in services. In other words, a population needs a service that is not available to them. The data for a need statement should come directly from a target group that is already receiving services. For example, a recreation program is working with a group of youth, but most of them have trouble getting to events because they do not have access to public transportation, and their parents cannot provide rides. This is a need. Need statements require people data that focuses on a specific population.

When writing a need statement, provide a brief, general overview of the problem, but make your request specific to the needs of your population. When writing a problem statement, keep in mind that it should be more global because problems (as defined here) concern more than one population and its need.

For program planners and developers, a lack of knowledge about the nature of a problem or need is an obstacle. But it is an obstacle that can be eliminated by acquiring a thorough familiarization with the problem. Start doing this by first documenting the problem or need, and then find out why it exists. Find out, from the community at large, what their understanding is of its causal factors. Look for any empirical data to support the existence of the identified problem or need.

In conjunction with determining the nature of the problem, attention should also be given to the effects of the problem. Do not be presumptuous in this determination, because it varies widely from community to community. For instance, in one community the problem of teenagers becoming sexually active in higher numbers may result in more teenage pregnancies; in another it may result in a greater high school dropout rate for female students; and in still another, a higher incidence of sexually-transmitted diseases.

When a proposal discusses the nature of a problem and its effects, this demonstrates to the funding source that an organization has a thorough understanding of it.

Be careful to not overstate your problem so that it is perceived by a funder as beyond the ability of your agency to tackle it, or beyond the agency's mission statement.

The problem or needs statement should also give direction for planning and implementing program activities. (These aspects of the proposal will be discussed in more detail later in this chapter.)

Another important aspect of problem identification, and one I discuss with clients and workshop participants, is "systems thinking." To solve problems, particularly social problems, program developers, planers, and administrators must use a systems approach.

The systems approach focuses on the interrelationships between internal and external structures. The selection of the population to be served, available technology, and managerial knowledge in an organization are all internal variables within an organization that can affect a program plan. Together they form an internal structure. However, there are also external variables that when combined form an external structure. These include such things as well-paying jobs, affordable housing, and resources for schools in a community. They can also affect the outcome of the *same* program plan. When developing programs to help fulfill a community's needs, organizations must understand the interrelatedness between these two structures, and this understanding should be reflected in all aspects of its program plan.

Fritjof Capra, a systems theorist and bestselling author, tells us, "The more we study the major problems of our time, the more we come to realize that they cannot be understood in isolation. They are systems problems...interconnected and interdependent."

When program developers factor into their problem solving how both internal and external structures influence our behaviors and thinking, they are systems thinkers. They can thereby see more clearly how to develop programs that can change behaviors. These programs will then be more effective at helping individuals and communities to avoid problems, not just applying quick-fix solutions that produce cures worse than the disease.

Peter Senge, director of the Center for Organizational Learning at MIT's Sloan School of Management, also examines the often hidden influence our systems have over us. In his book ***The Fifth Discipline***, he fully explores how systems and structured behaviors affect both our creative and analytical decision-making on different levels. What follows are some brief caveats he espouses that may be helpful to program developers. Here they are presented somewhat in isolation, so some of their significance may be diminished. To fully understand the thinking behind them and their ramifications, they need to be examined in a contextual sense. For that, I suggest you read Senge's book.

1. Today's problems come from yesterday's "solution."
2. The harder you push, the harder the system pushes back.
3. Behavior grows better before it grows worse.
4. The easy way out usually leads back in.
5. The cure can be worse than the disease.
6. Faster is slower.
7. Cause and effect are not closely related in time.
8. Change can produce big results; the areas of highest leverage are often the least obvious.
9. You can have your cake and eat it too, but not both at once.
10. Dividing an elephant in half does not produce two small elephants.
11. There is no blame.

Finally, another common mistake I have seen made by program planners and developers is using the problem or needs statement to justify a method or strategy. An agency will already have in mind what it wants to do and will use the problem or needs statement to document their approach. They combine the solution or method with the problem. When this occurs, a problem or needs statement might read like this: Male students in ABC middle school do not have appropriate role models. (Where do you think I'm going with this?) Consequently, they become involved with such antisocial behaviors as illegal drug use, gang activity, and violent conduct overall. A mentor program will. . . . Get the point? Remember, at this stage of the proposal, a problem or need is being documented, not *a method or solution*. Not having an appropriate role model is not a problem. It is a causal factor that may contribute to a problem, but it itself is not a problem.

Program Objectives

The need for well-written objectives has increased over the last few years. Most funding sources now require that all program evaluations have clearly measurable outcomes. Measurable outcomes are determined when writing objectives. Far too often, program developers and proposal writers confuse objectives with methods. A program objective describes what differences are anticipated because of your efforts. The *way* your objectives are accomplished is your method. A program objective must meet the following criteria:

1. Must be measurable. A program objective must include a quantitative amount of anticipated change, whether the change is an increase or decrease.
2. Must be time limited. There must be a target date when the anticipated change will have taken place.
3. Must be stated as an outcome. The objective must state an outcome: By training 35 volunteers (the method), we will reduce the incidence of illiteracy by 10 percent.
4. Must be relevant. The identified problem is adolescent alcohol and drug use, but the

program objective speaks of increased self-esteem. To be relevant, the objective has to solve the problem of adolescent alcohol and drug use.
5. Must be realistic. The program must be statistically able to function with the available resources. If your program is only going to work with 100 people, to say that unemployment in the county will be reduced by 10 percent is unrealistic.

Big numbers may look and sound impressive, but do not try to impress the funding source with unrealistic numbers. Proposal readers, especially those working with government agencies, are knowledgeable in the program area they are reviewing. Stretching the truth can damage your credibility.

Unfortunately, some funding sources may be misled and give credibility to an unreliable outcome because it is presented by an institution or group that has credibility in other areas. For instance, a university once wrote an objective that claimed it would decrease drug use by 50 percent over a one-year period. This is not very likely. However, because a *university* said it could do that, some of the proposal readers assumed the proposal writers knew what they were talking about. They believed the objective even though there was no empirical data to support the claim. An unrealistic outcome was given more credence than it deserved based solely on the fact it was made by a university. This kind of trickery may get your program funded, but when the anticipated outcomes are disappointing, similar programs (alcohol and drug programs in that case) are short changed. Another pitfall to doing this is even though the next program you submit to the same funder may be more viable, to them it may appear less credible. Another thing, funding sources do communicate with one another about the reputations of organizations, so facts about your unreliability can spread to other funders.

If a funding source asks about a project goal, it is usually requesting a purpose or mission statement about the intent of the program. For example, some government agencies set a goal for each program funded because it is a legislative mandate for disbursement of some public funds. Let us say a law is passed. It talks about better education for all children, but its stated goal is to increase the math scores of all public school eighth graders in the United States. This is a broad, general statement about the overall aim of the project--a goal. As stated, it does not meet the criteria of being measurable or time-limited, nor is it stated as an outcome, so it is clear to see it is not an objective. In my experience, this type of goal is not evaluated. If a goal is to be evaluated, it must meet the same five criteria as an objective.

At the end of this section is an exercise on differentiating methods from objectives. Take a few minutes to answer the questions. The right answers follow. Also, since this is an exercise that I use in the program planning trainings I do, you may find it to be a useful assessment tool if you work with a proposal writing team. It provides a quick way to determine the ability to fine objectives by all those involved with a proposal writing process, and then any misconceptions they may have about goals and objectives can be cleared up.

Methods

The method section describes the activities you plan to do to achieve the program objectives. It outlines the strategies that will be used to accomplish the outcomes. After reading this section, the funding source should know that your agency has the capability to accomplish its objectives. You must also convince a potential funder that your methods are appropriate for what you want to do.

More so than with any other part of the proposal, proposal writers usually demonstrate they are most comfortable writing about methodology. This is probably because here is where they get to layout their plans for fulfilling the vision they have for making things better. This is the section where they create activities that lead directly to solving an ill they have identified. However, no matter how passionately you feel about a specific activity, you must guard against overwhelming the readers with information about it. Be brief, clear, and specific. Do not write all your thoughts about the project in this section (nor any other part of the proposal), but make sure you tell funders what they need to know.

Including information such as the following when discussing your methods will help convince the funder your agency has enough information

about the activities you are proposing to address the identified problem:
- Other agencies with a similar target population that have used your selected approach.
- If available, scientific data to support your selected method.
- If what you are proposing is a model program of some reliable source such as a government agency, use this fact to support why the approach you've selected has a reasonable chance of working.
- A description of the program participants and the criteria you will use for selecting them for inclusion in the program.

Specificity and clarity are crucial to this section. Separate your methods into the specific tasks they entail in order for the activity to take place. For example, do not send out a proposal that discusses advertising employment training services but does not indicate when the advertisement will go out or the tasks that will be performed, and by whom, to get it out.

Requirements

What follows is some additional information relating to program implementation that should be shared with your potential funder. By making sure to provide details on these items, you're giving funders specifics about the people, tools, and climate needed to ensure the activities will be done. Specifically, when considering program requirements, keep in mind that they may cost money, and that should be factored in when determining costs associated with doing the program; delineate them in the program budget.

Personnel: What are the personnel needs and skills required to carry out the proposed program effectively? Are individuals available in your geographic area who can fulfill your personnel needs? If not, can individuals be enticed to consider moving to your area? What will it cost to find people with the skills needed to carry out the proposed program?

Training: If skilled personnel are not found, can people be trained to do the job? Is there a training source in your area? If not, where is one available? How much will this training cost, and is it reasonable to request funding for it? When trained, will those trained be able to train others, or can others be trained by the same outside source the initial personnel was trained by? Will training be an ongoing expense in order to maintain the project? Training may be needed for volunteer staff as well as paid staff.

Facilities and Equipment: Will additional facilities be needed to carry out the program? If so, are they available? What are your options if a facility is not available? Will vehicles, office furniture, communication systems, or any other special equipment be needed? What are the costs, and are they reasonable for a request? Is having these funds before your program is even set up necessary?

Political Environment: Deciding if your area is ready for a program is important. No matter how good an idea is, if the community-- and sometimes the target group--is not ready to participate in the program, it will fail! This happens often because the program idea is not consistent with the values and beliefs of the community. If a read of the political environment indicates resistance to your program, you must rally support by conducting public education activities. These activities should focus on defining the problem and presenting your organization's solutions. Only after the community takes ownership of the problem and solution, can the program work. Costs may also be incurred with this activity, and since this is a pre-program activity, your agency probably won't be able to get reimbursement for it from the funding source. It may be appropriate to seek funds from other sources for these activities.

Credibility: Yes, credibility is always important. Sometimes, as addressed previously under "Political Environment," people in a community may not be ready for a program when your organization is. They may not be ready because your organization is not credible in their eyes. When planning a program for an area that is geographically unfamiliar or is outside your established mission, conduct public relations activities before becoming too involved with program development. The community's perception of your organization and its plan will play a large role in the success of your program.

Other Considerations: These are logistical types of things that you may want to address in your proposal because they may peek a funder's curiosity. They include such things as area transportation systems, economic conditions, and age of participants. The effect crime and violence in certain areas may have on the success of a program may also have to be touched on. There are measures that can circumvent concerns like these, so make sure you address them in your proposal. For instance, do not plan activities that require transportation for participants in an area where privately-owned vehicles are not common without including provisions for transporting people. Planning evening activities in a community with a high crime rate is also not wise. In the same vein, you may not want to schedule activities on winter evenings in a northern state where participants may regularly have to drive in inclement weather.

Other Information

You may need to include resumes of the project's key staff with your proposal. For the sake of uniformity and neatness, use one format for all resumes and limit each to a page or two. Besides the individuals' work experience and education, include information related to the request, such as publications they've written and other professional endeavors. Carefully review and edit each resume.

This will help you to weigh whether or not the resumes you are presenting call attention to issues a potential funder may have strong feelings about. Some such issues are abortion, guns, capital punishment, and the medicinal use of marijuana. No matter how objective the review process may be, proposal readers will still bring their "personal baggage" into the process. This is not to imply that a reviewer would deliberately take points off because of a philosophical or political difference, but since all of us have values, beliefs, and opinions that influence us subconsciously, it is wise to delete controversial references. Also, I am not suggesting that you delete such things when they are relevant to your request.

Submitting time charts with foundation grants is not always necessary, but government grantors generally require them. If required to submit one, draw up a detailed step-by-step timetable that includes activities and tasks. This chart should be easy-to-understand so a reader can quickly find target dates for starting and completing activities. Make sure these time lines are reasonable, because oftentimes a reader may have been involved in a similar activity and may question too short or too long time allocations.

After reading this section, the funding source should know that you are capable of achieving your objectives because you know what you are doing and also because you have included reliable information to support you proposed methods.

Selecting the Method

Program methods and activities should not be decided on from hearsay or chance conversations with colleagues, friends, or associates. Method selection should be based primarily on what is known about the target group and its environment. Previous programs and other economic and cultural factors must also be considered.

If all these factors are taken into consideration, the one-size-fits-all approach to program planning and development (so popular in this country) will not work. The United States is too large and too diverse for this approach to solving problems or addressing needs. Model programs are good tools, but experience has taught me that they do not always work for all people, especially people who are outside societal norms. Differences exist within, and between, racial, ethnic, and religious groups. There is more than one way to be Mexican, Chinese, African, Australian, or Pacific Islander. There is more than one way to be Christian, Moslem, Buddhist, or Jewish. Differences influence outcomes. A program planner who gets excited about the notion of developing one program that would be effective for everyone everywhere strongly needs to question such an assessment. (Most likely the ego has something to do with this, but I'll save that discussion for another book.) When considering an evaluated or exemplary program model with proven results, use the model, but make adaptations designed to meet the needs of your target population.

Another consideration when selecting a model program is to make sure it has been rigorously evaluated by standard research techniques. Public agency funding sources have at times promoted "exemplary programs" that have not had a summative or outcome evaluation. Sometimes, for political reasons, a model without the approval of a knowledgeable person is given the designation "exemplary program."

Before choosing any method or approach, determine its relationship to your target group and its community. Ask yourself the following questions:

1. Why do we think this approach will work?
2. Do we have enough information to decide?
3. Has it been used with clients similar to ours?
4. Has it ever been conducted in a similar environment?
5. Is the organization that set up the program similar to ours?
6. Is it possible to talk to the staff and clients of the program that used it?
7. Was the political environment a factor in its effectiveness?

Knowing the details about the political environment surrounding an exemplary program is particularly important to your planning. Sometimes write-ups about an exemplary program do not mention that it took eight years to get the community to accept the particular program methods. There is no mention that the program organizers spent years educating people about the problem or that two project directors lost their jobs due to their inability to accomplish the delineated objectives. Knowing the history of the political environment in which the project was hatched is important. It is important because your program's effectiveness may depend on that knowledge.

Also when adapting a model program, consider carefully the data you collected during your needs assessment, so as to factor in information on the cultural and ethnic mix of your target population. Compare the economic factors. What may work in a middle-class community may not work in a low-income community. A program that works in an urban community must be modified if it is to work in a rural community. Remember, the United States is a large, economically and culturally diverse country. In recognition of that diversity, even McDonald's and Kentucky Fried Chicken allow franchise owners flexibility regarding products and services. For example, those who have visited Hawaii know that McDonald's offers Portuguese sausage on their breakfast menu. This is not available in Chicago, or Walla Walla, I would guess. Other factors to consider are age, gender, sexual orientation, and types of disabilities.

Evaluation

I will devote more attention to program evaluation than to the other segments of the proposal in this section because it continues to grow in importance. And with government requests, this may be an understatement because the evaluation component may often determine whether your project gets funded. The majority of questions I receive from clients and workshop participants are about some aspect of evaluation, and I find that people often are resistant to incorporating new information in this area.

Each director on a board, each staff person, each volunteer in an organization wants to know whether he or she is successfully carrying out the program mission and making a difference with clients. The results of an evaluation should show whether an effort is having a positive or negative effect on the targeted community. When an evaluation is an integral part of a program rather than just an afterthought, it can be an important tool for the ongoing improvement of the quality of the program's activity. Results from evaluations are more likely to be used if at the program planing stage staff play a part in shaping the evaluation process. Here are some reasons to conduct an evaluation:

1. To determine the effectiveness of a program;
2. To document that program objectives have been met;
3. To provide useful information about service delivery to program staff and other audiences; and,
4. To enable program staff to make changes that improve program effectiveness.

Evaluation and accountability are often linked together. Evaluations advance accountability and determine whether a program makes a difference. Accountability and making a difference are points that continue to grow in importance for funding sources and the public. In times of limited resources (which is most of the time) "evaluation" can be a threatening word to organizations hard pressed for funds, but evaluations must not be looked at as a service that is performed exclusively for keeping a funding source satisfied. Equally important is that evaluations can demonstrate your commitment to your clients and the community.

Evaluation: What it Entails

Evaluation is the systematic collection and analysis of data needed to make decisions. Evaluation is collecting and using information to answer questions about program effectiveness. It is a management tool that most well-run programs employ. Ideally, it starts at the program planning stage and continues as a significant activity throughout the proposal process and the life of the program itself. The following evaluation activities are a part of the program planning and should be incorporated into the operation of your program:

1. **Identifying the services needed.** This includes finding out what knowledge, skill, attitude, or problem behavior a program should address;
2. **Establishing program objectives.** This involves choosing the evidence (specific knowledge, attitudes, and behaviors) that will help determine fulfillment of the objectives. The first step to successful evaluation is a set of program objectives that meet the five criteria for a well-

written and well-developed objective. (See the five criteria in the Program Objectives segment.)
3. **Developing or selecting alternative program approaches**. This entails discussing and trying out various methods and techniques during program implementation to decide which are the most feasible and least costly.
4. **Monitoring program methods**. This involves setting up a management information system that shows who gets what services and how much they receive, as well as how participants rate those services. This also includes trying different program designs and determining how faithfully a particular approach is being implemented or to what extent it attracts and keeps participants.

A program administrator can determine from those activities what services to offer or how well services are being delivered. By incorporating them in the program planning process, it makes it easier for staff, directors, and funding sources to assess the effectiveness of a program's activities on a continual basis.

There are two broad classes of evaluations: formative or process evaluations and summative or outcome evaluations. Select the type of evaluation to use according to the needs of the agency, its clients, and other beneficiaries, as well as the requirements of the funding source. When making the selection, keep in mind you must factor in the availability of personnel and all other needed resources. Detailed information on both classes of evaluations follows.

Formative or Process Evaluation

Formative or process evaluations describe and assess program activities. Examining the achievement of program activities and documenting what has taken place in a program is important: Who did what to whom and for how long? The questions that must be answered are as follows:

1. Did the agency do what it said it was going to do?
2. Did it do it at the level projected? If not, why not?
3. Were activities carried out within the budget?
4. Did they use funds in the manner stated in the proposal?

Monitoring what a program does, money spent, and resources used are the basic ingredients of a process evaluation. For example, the program plan states that your organization will conduct three workshops on parenting within the first six months of your program's set up. At least 50 parents will attend each session, and each session will be four hours long. There will be three different site locations within the target area, and a Mandarin-speaking instructor will be at one site. The workshop curriculum will include how to conduct a family meeting, set rules for children, and improve intra-family communications. Each workshop instructor will be licensed by an accredited source.

After the workshops have taken place, evaluate the major assertions of the program plan:

1. Did 50 parents attend each workshop? If not, why not?
   a. Was it location?
   b. Was it subject matter?
   c. Was it marketing?
2. Were the sessions four hours long? If not, why not?
3. Did workshops take place at three sites?
   a. Was there a Mandarin-speaking instructor at one of the sites?
   b. If not, why not?
4. Did the workshop cover the curriculum stated in the program plan? If not, why not?
5. How did the participants feel about the workshop?
   a. What did they think about the environment?
   b. What did they think about the content?
6. Can you document that the instructors had parent training credentials from an accredited source?
7. What was the cost of each workshop?

a. Was the cost within the projected cost?
b. Did you have unexpected costs?

Summative or Outcome Evaluations

Summative or outcome evaluations assess program achievements and effects. Outcome evaluations study the immediate or direct effects of the program on participants and other beneficiaries: Will participants be able to communicate effectively, plan family meetings, and set rules after completing the four-hour parent workshops? The outcome evaluation examines not only new attitudes or knowledge gained but also the effects the program has on behavior.

If your overall program outcome is to have a measurable impact on a target group within a definite time period, use a summative evaluation. It will document the levels at which change occurred and determine if change took place because of your program. Greater detail about evaluation techniques and research methods will be needed if your project is very large. Data may be quantitative. For example, with a high school, it can compare the number of program participants to meals served, or the decrease in burglaries to the increase in reading scores. Qualitative information might detail what took place at a series of coalition meetings or training events. All evaluations use data collected systematically.

The evaluation essentially identifies whether the program plan, with the money and resources allocated, did the job it was designed to do. It can also determine whether the program has had an impact on participants, beneficiaries, and their environments. And during the program planning process, it is the first chance to look at possible program outcomes.

The following checklist will be helpful for planning an evaluation and reviewing the key steps of program planning and development.

Checklist for Planning an Evaluation

1. Are all methods, activities, and tasks **clearly described?**
2. Are there **defined program objectives?**
3. Are these program objectives **consistent** with the problem or need?
4. Do program staff and policymakers agree that these program objectives are **realistic?**
5. Do program activities and objectives have **continuity?**
6. Have all **program components** been identified?
7. Are there valid, **measurable** indicators for each program objective?
8. Is it **financially** feasible to collect these data?

9. Is all program staff **clear on what kind of information** the evaluation will provide?
10. Is there a plan for how program staff and administrators will **use and distribute the evaluation results** to modify the program?

Working with an Evaluator

First you have to find an evaluator. Preferably, choose an evaluator who has been referred to you by a satisfied colleague or another agency that has a similar mission to yours. A referral from a credible person or agency will save you time. If this avenue doesn't pan out, then check with colleges and universities in your area for evaluators. Look particularly for those who are national experts in your field.

Ideally from the planning stage, an evaluator should have input in the development of the evaluation as it relates to the selected activities. This helps agencies to avoid evaluation pitfalls that may not be obvious to program planners. Although, it is not always feasible for a person with such expertise to be available to you, and the main reason for this is cost. Whether your selected evaluator will be a subgrantee or an independent contractor, he/she will want to be paid as soon as he/she begins working on the plan. Of course, you're not funded yet, so this is a problem.

Explain to your evaluator that he/she will be a program evaluator and that his/her assistance in the program planning stage is an expectation of any of the program's subgrantees and independent contractors. Assure your evaluator of your good intentions by developing a memorandum of understanding and giving him/her a copy of it. The absolute latest your evaluator should begin working is the beginning of the funding period.

For the Proposal

Tell what kind of evaluation will be conducted. Discuss what kind of information will be collected, and how it will be used in making program modifications. Most government proposals require some discussion of not only what data will be collected but also on *how* it will be collected.
    The credentials of evaluators outside your project will be important to the funding source. Document each evaluator's experience, expertise, and objectivity. Explain why and how each person was selected. Include the selection criteria and a brief description of the process. If an evaluator is selected without competitive process, still discuss selection criteria. Criteria are needed whether there is a competitive process or not.

Future Funding

This section has always been important when requesting funds from foundations. Now it is even more important to public sources that want to know how your program will continue without their funds. Do not look at a foundation or public agency as a long-term funding source for a program. While an agency may have a relationship with a funding source, it will probably not be for the same program. Do not expect to receive funding for any one project from one foundation longer than two or three years.

Future funding is often the most neglected section of proposals. It should be discussed during program planning but rarely is. For your project to operate continuously, program personnel and board members must consider sources of future funding. Future funding prospects will affect the methods you choose for conducting activities and the program budget.

Your potential funding source, particularly private ones, will want to know what other source of funding your organization is exploring now, and also which ones you are exploring for future funding when the current budget is exhausted. Being able to provide this information signifies your agency has the wherewithal to continue the program's efforts in the future.

Is it reasonable for a funding source to fund an organization that cannot give a viable plan for continuation of the program after the initial funding period? Not if the funding source is expecting that even without their support the program will continue. Any program that needs more than a year or two to accomplish its outcomes must immediately make sure their planning strategy is in sync with the funding source's expectations. Since this is a development issue, what better time to start than in the planning stage.

In her book *Understanding Nonprofit Funding and Managing Revenue in Social Services and Community Development Organizations*, Kirsten A. Gronbjerg, sociology professor at Loyola University, Chicago, reveals that foundations are among the least stable and dependable sources of funding in the not-for-profit sector. Also in this book is her analysis of a study she did of 13 social service and community development organizations in Chicago, where she analyzed the effect foundation funding had on their stability. One of her observations was that foundations are transient entities in the lives of not-for-profits. She points out that foundations often have a taste for novelty and change that can create problems when an organization is seeking continuous funds to survive.

I feel very strongly about this issue. It is an important aspect to consider because of the responsibility an organization has to its clients and constituents. On too many occasions, I have observed that programs that started because money was available were forced to close a year or two later because additional funds were not available. In several cases, clients and the community had become dependent on the much needed services they provided. There were times when I thought it better to do nothing than to accept funds that would end and leave the community worse off after the program failed. People of color and low communities have been particularly affected by this scenario.

It is irritating to me to get telephone calls from individuals telling me their funding source is cutting or eliminating their funding. However, this is usually distorted information. After I ask a few questions, it usually comes out that the situation is not as first explained. The real scenario is that their funding will cease on a date they have known of for a year or more. So it is even more annoying to me that I've received such a call for assistance only weeks before a grant is supposed to end.. (Yes, I do know that funds are sometimes unexpectedly cut. While writing this book, some agencies whose funding was cut by one year came to my attention.) Not-for-profit organizations will always have to raise funds, so why not incorporate an ongoing process for generating funds into the structure of the organization? I still know executive directors who talk about "getting one big grant" so they will no longer have to keep writing proposals and soliciting funds. It is foolish to long for something like this. The chances of it happening are akin to winning over a million dollars in a state lottery. Fundraising, like having to generate money to live on, is a continuous process. Prepare for it!

The discussion of future funding should not be limited to grant support. Plan to explore various income options that might be open to organizations such as yours. Consider the commitment and willingness of your organization's board of directors to involve themselves in fundraising. The membership of the board will also have some bearing on your ability to look at non-grant possibilities. If the board consists primarily of individuals employed by other 501(c)(3)s, they may not be able to help with some of your fundraising activities because of formal or informal restrictions placed on them by their employers. Most often these restrictions stem from loyalty issues because their employers may be seeking funds from the same sources yours is. Consequently, a board should not be comprised mostly of individuals from other 501(c)(3), non-for-profit, organizations. I will talk more about this in the chapter on boards of directors.

Is there a cadre of volunteers who can help along with your board of directors in fundraising events? A successful fundraiser should take up little, if any, staff time. Fundraising is the responsibility of the board of directors. The board has a legal responsibility to keep the doors of the organization open. While they may delegate part of this responsibility to the staff, they cannot abdicate it completely.

Consider your visibility and reputation. If your organization enjoys high visibility but poor reputation, fundraising attempts will be futile. This must be rectified. Improving your service and product will help to enhance your reputation. Improve the quality of your service quickly while gradually increasing your public image. When your agency has low visibility and a good reputation, conducting public relations activity before fundraising efforts will be helpful. Be honest when assessing your visibility and reputation quotient. Conduct interviews with staff, and also survey clients, other agencies, and community leaders.

What follows are some questions I ask clients when planning to incorporate future funding efforts with program planning activities:

1. Can you charge fees for your services? If not, why not? Have you explored this as an option?
2. Can you solicit donations from individuals and/or develop an annual donor program? If not, why not? Have you explored this as an option?
3. Can you solicit contributions from previous clients or alumni? If not, why not? Have you explored this as an option?

4. Can you develop a special event fundraiser? Have you explored this as an option? If not, why not?
5. Is some type of third-party payment possible? Have you explored this as an option? If not, why not?

These suggestions are tried and proven. Granted, they may not be appropriate choices for all programs or agencies, but it still surprises me that most agencies I work with have not explored any of these possibilities. Many of these organizations and their boards are so grant driven that they refuse to look at other options. And they are doing themselves a great disservice if they think they should receive a grant simply because they exist.

I know income derived from non-grant sources may not support a program or an organization's operating budget, but demonstrating to funders the organization has the ability to acquire these dollars can be leverage for receiving more dollars, and even more grants. The day is coming when agencies *will have to* demonstrate a capacity for fund development, particularly with private funders. At that time, many agencies will not survive unless they have a diversified funding base that includes some non-grant support.

As I was working on this book, the Substance Abuse and Mental Health Services Administration (SAMHSA) and the Center for Substance Abuse

Prevention announced many program cuts. (This occurred in many federal agencies. I just happen to know more about these two.) This action subsequently eliminated programs before funding periods ended. The budgets were reduced for many communities, public housing authorities, and schools. Their clients and communities lost services, but what also can't be ignored is the disruption in the lives and families of people working in those programs. During this time, I was working with an agency that was anticipating cuts in its budget. Stress and anxiety gripped staff and board members. It is not as if the people at SAMHSA deliberately set out to wreck people's lives. The choices were few. Congress appropriated only so many dollars for SAMHSA--in this case $218 million, short of the $346 million required to meet all its commitments to grantees. It was a congressional decision and to some degree that means the decision of "we, the people." After all, this is a democracy. As a result of such great reductions in funds, though, more and more funding sources are deciding to eliminate funding rather than cut each of their programs to the point that delivering quality programs is nearly impossible. This is what SAMHSA did. Instead of making across-the-board cuts, they eliminated some programs and reduced funding in others.

Around this time, the United Way of the San Francisco Bay Area also eliminated or drastically cut many organizations from its funding list. This was a radical departure from the funding patterns of previous years. The disbursement of their $17.6 million community impact funds was drastically altered. Funding to long-term beneficiaries like the Salvation Army was cut down to $70,000 from $363,000. The San Francisco Girl Scouts Council funding went from $30,000 down to $22,874. Several YMCAs and YWCAs were not funded. Formerly *guaranteed* funds, for organizations such as Camp Fire Boys and Girls and the Bay Area Urban League, were dropped. However, 106 never-before-funded programs and organizations received funding for the first time. Two hundred fifty-one programs out of an original list of 1700 received funds. The overall number of programs funded by this United Way affiliate dropped from 850 to 350.

As I travel around the country, I hear complaints about the local United Way and its perceived obligation to fund a core group of organizations. Through changing the list of organizations selected for funding, the San Francisco affiliate changed the paradigm and opened opportunities to some lesser known organizations and groups not connected with national organizations. Its officials have explained this shift by saying they were emphasizing "results-oriented" community services. This shift is especially worth paying attention to because California--to the chagrin of some--is a trend setting state. Many things that have wide application have started here: Bluejeans, personal computers, the lust for bottled water. As such, I have observed that this funding pattern is now a growing trend nationally.

Also, despite its recent problems nationally, United Way enjoys high credibility and is a powerful influence in the philanthropic community. So look out for similar actions in other funding sources, not just United Way.

Fundraising can also play a significant role in an agency's marketing and public relations efforts. It is a great way to increase your supporters and your financial health. Take this opportunity to remind the community and others of your organization's existence and beneficial work in the community. It is also an ideal way to get the leaders from various segments of your community involved with your project. Gala events such as dances, auctions, and dinners are good ways to network, have fun, and raise money. Community members can participate in an agency's work and even take credit for some parts of it.

The more money your organization can raise from the local community, the stronger it will be. Fundraising empowers an organization in a way that grants cannot. Getting lazy is easy for an organization when the organization has grants. Fundraising keeps your group involved with people and the community and forces the organization to expand its support base.

Clearly, you will always have to write grants. Most 501(c)(3)s are not going to survive without them, but they also need to find other ways to raise funds. Anne Firth Murray of the Global Fund for Women says, "...it is through diversity that one learns and is able to gain access to different funding sources. It is essential that in a fundraising plan there be built-in goals for obtaining funds from several different sources."

Andy Robinson, author of *Grassroots Grants: An Activist's Guide to Proposal Writing,* recommends that at least half an agency's budget come from individuals, major donors, benefits, and earned income. A more realistic percentage for the agencies I work with is one-third. But either percentage will make an excellent outcome for an agency's five- or ten-year-fund-development plan. Annual outcomes might be 10 percent to 20 percent a year depending upon the number of years in the plan and the organization's capability.

I recommend every organization I counsel to ask itself two important questions: first, does your community know your organization and what it does? Often agency staff is not sure how the community views it and its efforts. Has your agency done anything in the last six months that would make the community know that it is there? The second--and most important--question is: does your community know how it benefits from your work? If the community does not know how it benefits from your services, how will it know to support your work financially or any other way? A successful agency will develop a public relations or marketing plan that will keep the community informed of its actions and how those actions benefit the community's members.

Budget

The budget should reflect the projected costs of the program. This section of the proposal should delineate each specific item of the budget. When clients ask how detailed the budget should be, I say it should include details for all projected expenditures. Every line item should have an explanation for how the figures were derived. For example, in the line item for equipment, identify and account for every chair, desk, file cabinet, computer, printer, and every other unit of equipment. Besides a detailed budget, most government grants will request a budget narrative that describes each line item. Write a narrative even when there is no requirement, especially for those items that are unusual and are not self-explanatory.

Should the budget be inflated or padded, is often the next question. Proposal writers sometimes inflate financial figures assuming the funding source only gives a percentage of any request. I do not recommend doing this. Besides, most funding sources can recognize an inflated budget, so doing so may cause them to question your integrity. Submit a planned and well-thought-out budget that is reasonable, realistic, and credible. This kind of budget gives you an opportunity to demonstrate your managing and fiscal planning abilities. If you cannot present an accurate budget, why should a funding source believe your organization can effectively manage their investment?

There are times when a funding source (in my experience, a local, public one) will reduce a budget to an amount that is unrealistic, making it impossible for the potential recipient to carry out the program effectively. Your group may be tempted to take what funds are offered, particularly if you are financially strapped, but be careful in these circumstances. Do not accept a grant so drastically reduced that your program cannot be effectively implemented. This would be a big mistake! An agency must be willing to say no to unrealistic cuts. Many funding sources will respect a refusal made on this basis and will give your future applications special consideration.

When developing your budget, contact various vendors to get accurate cost and pricing information. Ideally, get three estimates. Do not guess how much a product or service will cost. Another way to estimate costs is to check with similar organizations or agencies on their products, services, and costs for salaries and benefits. Organizations such as United Way often conduct salary surveys that include information from local not-for-profit organizations.

Budget development is almost an afterthought in many organizations, but I suggest you allow adequate time for this essential part of program planning. By the time the program planning is complete and the writing of the proposal begins, the budget should be fully developed. This should not have to be a major undertaking, because costs for carrying out all activities, purchasing materials, paying staff, and other required expenditures should be assessed throughout the planning process. Funding sources want to see a fully justified and realistic budget, and the requesting agency should be willing to comply. Not just for them, but also for its own planning purposes.

You should be aware of the effect the Fair Labor Standards Act can have on your budget. Will the program use nonexempt employees who will work overtime? If the answer is yes, you may want to include overtime pay with the wage and salary allocations. Government agencies, businesses, and all types of organizations violate this law by giving compensatory time to nonexempt employees rather than paying overtime. If an agency finds itself embroiled in a lawsuit with an employee over this issue, the burden of proof falls on the employer. In other words, an employee--usually a disgruntled one--can file a claim without having to provide proof. Every year over 93,000 claims are filed, and usually the employee, or former employee, gets a judgment in her/his favor. Protect yourself and your organization, get a copy of this law from your own state or the federal Department of Labor.

Personnel considerations and policies are important, because costs and expenses related to personnel make up a large percentage of budgetary expenditures. Fringe and health benefits, sick leave, and vacation time can destroy your budget if their costs have not been factored in. More than once I have worked with program developers and planners who never reviewed their agency's personnel policies while developing their budget. If your agency has wage and salary guidelines, be sure to review them and try to have positions classified, or at least tentatively classified, before submitting the proposal. This will allow you to submit better salary and wage cost information. Also, use an average of the entry level, midrange, and high-end salaries in determining the budget amount for each position. This will give you flexibility when hiring staff.

Procedure and operations manuals might dictate the use of independent contractors whenever possible to reduce wage costs. There may be jobs that do not require full-time nor part-time employees. The nature of the work may allow an agency to contract with an independent contractor. For example, a monthly or quarterly newsletter may be less costly and of better quality if produced by an independent contractor.

Sometimes organizations create positions that are next to impossible to fill. A program may need a part-time counselor. An agency manager decides to find someone who is not only a counselor but who is also able to write and produce a newsletter. Public relations activities are also indicated as part of the counselor's job description. This puts the agency in a situation where it will have to find someone able to counsel, write and produce a newsletter, and do public relations work. This is a difficult task. However, there are individuals in most geographic areas who can do public relations or produce the newsletter as an independent contractor for less than the costs involved in hiring a part-time employee. These costs are less because an independent contractor can be paid a flat rate. No allotments have to be calculated for fringe benefits, health benefits, vacation time, or sick leave.

Administrative costs are next to nothing for an independent contractor because there are no employee claims to process. The quality of work may also be better because you are using an individual with specialized skills. Lets face it, a position that requires unrelated skills may not manifest the highest quality work in every area.

Proposal writing, staff training, newsletter production, and public relations work are activities of an agency that do not require full-time employees. External consultants can be used as needed for organizational development activities, strategic planning, and evaluations. Independent contractors can also eliminate the stress that goes with the dreaded task of laying-off individuals when a grant concludes, and the agency has no alternative positions. (I know some of you know what I mean.)

I admit having a bias in favor of independent contractors. Not only do I often work as an independent contractor, but I am also involved with several organizations that use their services. This option is a productive, efficient, and cost-effective means for getting quality work.

When using an independent contractor, an organization should maintain policies and procedures that explain the process for selecting and relating to these individuals. Often, organizations want to treat them as employees, and they are not. A pamphlet is available from the Internal Revenue Service that lists 19 or 20 criteria that can be used to determine this status. The following six have been included here because they are the ones I deem most important in helping determine if the worker in question is an independent contractor or an employee.

1. First, independent contractors do not have supervisors. However, they are accountable for their performance and work. You should use written agreements clearly stating performance criteria, due dates, time lines, and contact persons with the contracting agency.

2. Independent contractors maintain their own schedule. They cannot be required to report to a particular site at eight o'clock, to take lunch at noon, a morning break, an afternoon break, or to leave at five o'clock.
3. Independent contractors do not have an office or permanent work station. They may use an office, but it is not their office; it is just a vacant or guest office.
4. Independent contractors are not eligible for fringe benefits and are liable for their own taxes. The agency does not arrange for tax withholding, payment of FICA, or Workers' Compensation Insurance. These items are the responsibility of the individual contractor. State this in the agreement.
5. Independent contractors must provide the resources needed to conduct the work. This does not mean they may not use some of the agency's materials, but for the most part, they provide their own equipment, supplies, and materials. This may mean costing out some items in the contract.
6. An independent contractor is free to do the same work for other organizations. In fact, ideally he or she should work for more than one client during a twelve-month period. If not, it could appear that an individual is really an employee. Public agencies in particular have had problems here because they would not allow an independent

contractor an opportunity to work for another agency. Not adhering to this criterion often gets agencies into trouble.

I have worked with public agencies that have used the term "consultant" as part of a job title, such as "health promotion consultant." Do not confuse using the word "consultant" in this way to necessarily mean that a person is an independent contractor. Somebody called a consultant, or anything else, can only be an independent contractor if they meet the Internal Revenue Service criteria. And the budget should indicate that such a person is an independent contractor, no matter what job title your agency may use when referring to them.

An agency should develop a procurement policy and use it in the budget development process. A procurement policy can be very helpful when negotiating or discussing costs and pricing information with funding sources. If the board of directors maintains a procurement policy, it shows that there is a process for selecting vendors. Having policies and procedures in place, gives fundseekers credibility with funding sources. It shows that there are internal fiscal controls.

Items in the budget should correspond with the proposal's narrative. The budget should be consistent with points in the proposal. Personnel line items should be consistent with the discussion of staff in the narrative. The budget should be consistent with the activities listed in the method section. For example, do not put an item in a budget for monograph development unless it is mentioned in the proposal.

If your organization is part of a larger agency, there will be indirect and overhead expenses. These are costs incurred by the larger agency within which your program operates. If that entity provides certain administrative services such as payroll, office space, equipment, and other services, including such costs in the budget is appropriate. The total of these expenses reflects the percentage your agency requests from a funder for indirect costs. If the proposed program or project is not part of a larger operation, there are no indirect costs.

Government contracts with larger agencies often refer to negotiated rates. These rates are the allowable percentage for indirect costs. Breaking out certain costs as line items is allowed. Some foundations and some state agencies do not recognize indirect costs. Do not confuse these costs with fees or payments for services that are performed as a part of conducting program functions and activities.

Proposal Summary

Most government agencies require an abstract or summary of the proposal. This statement appears on the first page, but it should be the last thing written. It should be no more than three-quarters of a page, or 30 to 35 lines when using a 12-point font. This abstract can set a tone that will determine the reader's perception of the proposed program and the requesting agency. It could play a role in determining whether the proposal is read with the first group of proposals or read toward the end of the process. The latter may not be good for your effort.

A proposal submitted to a foundation that is more than three or four pages should include a summary that contains a concise and brief description of material from each section of the proposal. It should identify the applicant and provide one or two sentences explaining why the applicant is credible. It should cite the major reason for the grant request, state the objectives, and describe the primary approach to the problem. The summary or abstract should also state the total cost of the project, committed funds, and the amount of the proposal request. This is a lot to convey in such a short summary, so choose your words carefully. Brevity and clarity will persuade the reader to read the rest of the proposal. Do not take the task of writing this section lightly. Do allow yourself enough time to write it. No matter how well thought out your program or how well written your proposal, someone has to read it. This section can determine if your proposal is read at all, and if it is well reviewed.

Exercise: Program Objectives and Outcomes

A program objective or outcome meets five criteria. It must be measurable, time-limited, stated as an outcome, and be realistic and relevant in relation to the problem or needs statement. The first three criteria are pertinent to this exercise. Which of the following are program objectives?

1. Eighty-five percent of 100 participants will increase their reading level two grade levels by June 30, 2001.
2. By June 30, 2001, at least 100 community residents will have an opportunity for employment because of the training program.
3. To train 200 students in communication skills and problem solving by June 30, 2001.
4. Increase the participants in the program by 25 percent by January 30, 2001.
5. One hundred youth from the eastside will have access to transportation to the youth center by June 30, 2001.
6. There will be a 5 percent decrease in alcohol and drug use among sixth-grade students in ABC Middle School within 30 months of starting the program.

Answers:
1. This is definitely a program outcome. It includes two measurements (85 percent and

two grade levels). June 30, 2001, is the time limitation, and it is stated as an outcome. The students will be reading two grade levels above their current level.
2. I hope you did not say that this is an objective, because it is not. Unfortunately, it is typical of the objectives I see in proposals. First, there is no measurement. Is *opportunity* measurable? Is the program about *jobs* or *opportunities for jobs*? If all program participants have an opportunity for employment, but none of them obtain an employer, would the program be successful? Is the program worth funding?
3. This statement is typical of what too many proposal writers and program developers still believe to be outcomes. The tip-off that this is not an outcome is the use of the infinitive "to" and the action verb "train." To train is a process. Doing something-- managing a program, teaching a class--is a process, and your outcome is the result of what you did. After training is complete, participants will be able to do what they cannot do now: get a job, read, or use a computer.
4. How about this one? It is not an outcome. *Why* is it that program personnel want to increase participation? *How* will their clients benefit? These questions are not answered.

5. See the above. Same issues.
6. This one is the best example of the six statements. It has a measurement, is time limited, and is stated as an outcome. Of course, we can debate the significance of the 5 percent outcome and the 30-month time limitation, but the significance of the numbers is not relevant to what we are trying to determine here. Although there is little specific information telling why this is a realistic outcome, this statement itself is appropriate for our criteria.

How did you do? Remember, your outcomes must fit with all other sections.

Who Are These People?

I have included the idea of "credibility" in every section of the process of proposal writing, but in this chapter I will discuss it in detail. It is a critical element that the proposal must establish to the satisfaction of the funding source.

The funding source needs to have a sense of who the requesting organization is, some of the areas it is involved in, and some the individuals associated with it. Some funding sources ask for this information in the what's called the "applicant agency," "organization capability," or "organization capacity" section. Other funding sources (and The Grantsmanship Center) prefer heading this section "Introduction." This section introduces the reader to the requesting organization and gives some rudimentary information about the request being made. Foundations usually require this information in a section at the beginning of the proposal. Government agencies request it in several places.

Documentation of your agency's activities, how information is presented, and everything written throughout the proposal is all part of your credibility quotient. Your agency's credibility is being scrutinized with your every contact with the funding source. Each meeting and every telephone conversation add to the picture being drawn of your organization.

Your proposal should not have credibility gaps. ***Webster's New World Dictionary, Second College Edition,*** defines a credibility gap this way: "An apparent disparity between what is said and the actual facts, or . . . the inability to have one's professed motives accepted as the true ones."

An organization may emphasize what it is going to do rather than its ability to get things done effectively. The proposal frequently has little information about the organization's track record. Why should a funding source be interested in your project without knowing anything about the organization? They will not be interested unless they are convinced of your program's soundness. Document your targeted population's need for your program. Convince the grantor that you can do what you say you can.

A source may believe your organization is competent and credible when it is not. A poor choice is sometimes made because a request is received from a high-profile organization with credibility in other areas. Consider this: An organization wants to start a program that falls outside its expertise or within a community where it has no experience. Its perceived credibility may sway a grantor, but, unfortunately, the target population will not get the help it needs. It is usually an affiliate of a national organization that benefits from such an erroneous perception.

Areas to Cover

Provide background information that includes the history of the organization; the agency's funding sources; and anything about its beginnings that may be significant to the request. The name of the agency may need an explanation if it is a person's name or does not identify what it does. For example, in my old hometown of Indianapolis, there is a social service organization named "Christmore House." What is a Christmore? Those not attending Catholic school or not having experience with Latin, may not know it means "for Love of Christ." And once they know that, they may be even more curious to know why such a name is attached to a secular organization.

The reason behind the organization's founding may be appropriate to mention. I have worked with several shelters for physically abused women. One such shelter was founded by a group of formerly abused women. When founders of this group were suffering abuse, shelters were nonexistent in their community, so they started a shelter.

One of my favorite stories is about the founding of a library in a small Idaho town. In the early 1950s, it seems there was no library there. The mothers in the community came together and decided to organize one for their children. Each mother donated 50 cents and committed herself to raise funds by participating in a white elephant sale of bric-a-brac and other inexpensive items. These proceeds and old books donated by town residents were the beginning of the town's public library system. To this day, the town mothers continue to have the annual white elephant sale. An interesting story can help engage the reader and give insight into an organization and its supporters.

The organization capability section can include information about the agency's mission, personnel, and board of directors. Include two or three sentences to profile some of your board members and staff. Focus on any activities they have been involved in that relate to similar interests the funding source has. In the appendix include a roster of your board members and other information to illustrate the board's accountability in carrying out its fiduciary responsibilities.

Include honors and recognition given to the organization, staff, and board members. Cite publications. Mention recent radio and television appearances. When this information is not current, make sure it is from valid sources, such as national magazines or network media.

Stress accomplishments of the organization's past or current programs. Use information from evaluations or statements from credible staff, community leaders, and other groups to cite the agency's successes (financial and otherwise). At one time, information of an organization's financial successes would have been something pleasant to give a funding source, but today it is essential. Your agency must show its fundraising or financial development capacity.

Sometimes agencies do not like to make funding sources aware of their successful fundraising abilities because they fear the source will conclude that financial assistance is not needed. I acknowledge that a few funding sources--usually at the local level--may penalize an organization for having this ability, but with most funders, your ability to raise money usually enhances your overall credibility. To make the point, if you are unemployed, borrowing from a lending institution can be nearly impossible, unless you possess valuable real estate or other substantial assets. The rule is the same when soliciting money from funding sources. An old axiom says it takes money to get money. This truism also applies to not-for-profits. It is no coincidence that financially well-to-do not-for-profits receive the largest number of grants and the greatest amount of money.

Your agency's inability to raise funds could keep funding sources and contributors from investing in your agency. A grantor might want to know why an agency that's a contributing member of the community cannot raise money in its own community. There will be more discussion of this subject later.

Most private funding sources ask the applicant to include audit and financial statements from a certified accountant. Foundations will also want to see the applicant's Internal Revenue Service 501(c)(3) determination letter. Occasionally public sources also require these items.

Community-based organizations and smaller agencies sometimes apply for foundation funding without having in place an annual budget nor audit and financial statements. If your agency is not a fully functioning organization, it needs a readiness plan for becoming one. A readiness plan must be set up before applying for foundation funding. It may be necessary to seek the services of a fiscal management consultant to help with this task.

Showing Your Credibility

The following list is adapted from information contained in The Grantsmanship Center's *Program Planning and Proposal Writing*. To enhance your funding opportunities, include in your proposal information on selected items from this list.

1. When, how, and why the organization was started; including information about the founder(s);
2. Organization mission statement, goals, and philosophy;
3. Important events in the organization's history;

4. Noteworthy programs, activities, and sponsorships, current ones and prior;
5. Program accomplishments and efforts, including financial accomplishments, include fundraisers and successful grant procurements;
6. Demographic characteristics regarding your clients and other constituents;
7. Assistance your organization has provided to other agencies at their request;
8. Referrals your agency has received to assist other groups in their delivery of services;
9. Noteworthy comments regarding the agency's work;
10. Results of any program evaluations, particularly outcome data;
11. Quotes from letters of support, clients, other agencies and experts in the field, and public figures (relating to the organization);
12. Invitations the agency has received to provide testimony on legislation, to appear on television or radio talk shows, or to speak at conferences (one or two examples of these would be included in an appendix);
13. Agency publications such as annual reports or newsletters (may be better to just quote from these documents);

14. Any other things that showcase your organization.

Remember, credibility is in the eye of the beholder. What may be creditable to one funding source may not be to another. Know your funding source and what captures their interest.

Your organization may have the longest, most glorious history imaginable, with volumes written about its effectiveness, but do not put all of it in a proposal. Trying to say everything risks boring the reader and losing a funding chance. Decide what is apt to be most persuasive and relevant to the reader.

To summarize, the applicant agency section establishes the agency's identity, qualifications, and credibility. This section must engage the reader. Call attention to your agency's strengths by giving specific information on things such as its proven program development track record, its available resources, its involvement with the community's recognized pillars, its ability to generate supplemental funds. Establish the reasonableness of the organization's mission. Then in a paragraph or two toward the end of the section, give a short overview of the program. This introductory information should be presented in a logical and sequential flow that puts the request in context with how the program will unfold.

Just Where is the Money?

Organizations I counsel and individuals who attend the classes that I conduct for The Grantsmanship Center are generally the least familiar with foundation funding and corporate philanthropy. Therefore, they are more interested in discussing these types of funding sources than public ones. The key to successfully soliciting funds from any source is to understand it.

Part of my purpose here is to demystify the nature of foundations as related to the proposal development process. Although foundation fund solicitation requirements and procedures vary, there are some elements common to every potential funder. Foundations reject some proposals because they do not meet their grant guidelines. Other proposals are rejected because the requesting agency is not prepared to meet foundation scrutiny. The first step to take when researching foundations is to decide whether their type of funding is appropriate for your agency and program. Even though money may be available for a particular cause, foundation or corporate funding is not ideal for all organizations. Later in this chapter I will cover some of the characteristics and funding criteria foundations have that will aid you in making this determination.

Some organizations and individuals apply for foundation funding because they have 501(c)(3) status. For example, a typical agency applying for private funding is as follows: This agency has nine employees, but no formal personnel policy. It has budgets for all of its programs, but there is no formal financial policy, statement, or procedure. Budgets for these programs have had a financial audit, but the agency has not. The agency board is not involved in any aspect of the agency's fund development efforts, not even contributing from their personal resources. These problems are common among organizations attempting to secure foundation funding. They have put these agencies in disarray, and their fund solicitation efforts will fail. A readiness plan is needed.

You will save frustration, disappointment, and time by honestly assessing your agency's readiness to pursue any private funding source. A solid readiness plan should include the following information and activities:

1. The history and development of all the agency's functions and activities;
2. Board activities and responsibilities;
3. Personnel policy development;
4. Program strategies;
5. Budget development plan;
6. Financial audit,
7. Fundraising activities.

If your organization is small or new, begin to look for funds at the local level when your readiness plan is complete. Funds can be sought from your constituents, community supporters, community businesses, faith groups, and civic and social clubs. Have a fundraiser. Foundations that consider funding an agency want to see evidence of local support, and some government agencies require a cash match.

The key to securing a foundation grant is finding a grantor that is compatible with your organization and its proposed program. The most common areas to look for compatibility in are geographic areas, the interests of the foundation related to the nature of your request, population groups, amount of request, and type of recipient. usually funded.

Contacting a foundation that does not fund in your geographical location or service delivery area is counterproductive. For example: A group from Dallas, Texas, was seeking funding for an art program in their city. They submitted a proposal to a foundation because they had heard it funded art projects. Their proposal was summarily rejected. Because they hadn't done the necessary research, they didn't know that foundation only funded art projects in New York City. Sometimes the situation is not so clear cut: An organization in a geographic area not funded by their targeted foundation is seeking funding for a program that will be set up in an area the grantor does fund. I would advise pursuing this grant. This is not a perfect match, but the organization and foundation could find ways to work with each other.

An organization seeking funding needs to know the interests of the foundation. Is it arts and humanities, community activism, cultural consideration, etc.? If your organization is seeking funding for a residential youth center, the funder must be interested in youth. If your group decides their community needs a residential care facility for young substance abusers, the foundation must be interested in funding both areas: youth and substance abuse. Your program has to match the interest of the funder.

The type of support your group is seeking has to match the type of support the grantor has a history of giving. Are you making a request for building renovation, or are you asking for program funds or seed money? If you have a request to finance the renovations of a facility, there is no need to approach a source that only funds programs. Seek those funders that fund renovations.

In the nonprofit world, like most other places, factors such as ethnicity, gender, class, or sexual orientation, influence decisions made about who gets funded. Let's say your community-based organization serves youth. The targeted foundation has a history of supporting youth activities. This may be a match. But keep considering. Your program specifically benefits gay and lesbian youths, and the targeted foundation has no history with gay and lesbian causes. This may not be a match because gay and lesbian causes are too controversial for some foundations. Unwillingness to fund controversial causes is not limited to foundations, even unbiased funders may surrender to societal pressures and walk away from any group or issue that is controversial. Information about a foundation's biases is difficult to find. Read between the lines.

The amount of the request is important. Your program request is for $100,000; the foundation's largest award in the past two years has been $15,000. No match here. Soliciting funds from several foundations that give matching grants is appropriate. However, it is not good form to take a $100,000 program to ten foundations and request $10,000 from each. Besides, even if the program were to be funded by such a strategy, having to answer to ten different foundations about one program would create an unbearable bureaucracy for most organizations.

The recipient of program services must be the type group that the funder usually funds. This criteria requires matching some key variables. Let us say your research leads to a funder that has a history of funding projects like yours, in your geographical area, and at the amount you are requesting. Five of six categories match. Your project is community based, concerned with the elderly living on an Indian reservation. Even though your program may line up with the foundation's funding preferences in some key categories, if there is no evidence that this organization funds *community-based groups*, this source is probably not a match. This is true even though it may have funded elderly Native Americans through community health centers operated by universities. What your group does, who the recipients of your efforts are, *and* the organizational category your group falls under all affect your chances of getting your program funded.

Although, don't rule this funder out completely. If your organization is credible and is supported by board members and staff who are involved with and committed to the health of Native Americans, this funding source might still be worth pursuing. You may be able to form a collaborative relationship with a university medical center or hospital in your area. Being able to demonstrate your agency has formed a collaborative partnership with the type organization a particular funder usually funds might increase your chances of success. In these times of cost-cutting measures, being able to form collaborations is becoming a necessary survival tactic for many organizations and businesses, big and small. To expound further on this, Warren Bennis and Patricia Ward Biedeman tell us in their book **Organizing Genius: The Secrets of Creative Collaboration**, "...in a global society in which timely information is the most important commodity, collaboration is not simply desirable, it is inevitable. In all but the rarest cases, one is too small a number to produce greatness."

Before approaching a foundation, conduct research to decide whether it is a potential funding source. Doing your homework will help assure that your proposal will be submitted to a compatible foundation. Foundations are different from each other in that they have distinct purposes, missions, and interests. Each will have different rules, requirements, and funding priorities that change from time to time.

Researching the Sources

The five Foundation Center libraries around the country provided one of the most complete data banks for researching foundations. The Center also has over 200 cooperating collections housed in public libraries. These facilities are an excellent place to begin your research. The Foundation Center gathers data and distributes reliable information on philanthropy. Contact the Center and ask to be put on the mailing list for the quarterly catalog. It has many directories and publications that are useful in researching foundations. A list of the cooperating collections is available by mail and online. There is no charge for the use of these libraries or cooperating collections. You may also find funding information at public libraries and organizations that are not a part of this extensive national network.

If you are serious about foundation funding, you must use the Foundation Center's services. I find several of the Center's publications extremely helpful. One of these is the **Foundation 1000**, which provides a comprehensive review of the 1000 wealthiest foundations in the country (according to their grant awards). Another helpful resource is *Grant Guides*, which is a collection of forty publications that target a variety of interests. These guides list recently awarded grants and show foundations interests. Descriptions are given of grants amounting to $10,000 or more. When I work with substance abuse prevention agencies, I use *Grant Guides* to obtain information about alcohol and drug abuse programs and health programs for children and youth. When working with programs involving people of color, I use *The Grant Guide for Minorities*.

When using Foundation Center publications for research, it is often necessary to use more than one book. This is a small drawback. One of the reasons I like *Foundation 1000*, though, is if you identify a potential funding source here, no other directory is needed. Most cooperating collections now also have the Foundation Center's CD-ROM.

Another source of foundation information is the Taft Group Publications. While the Taft Group does not have the vast network of The Foundation Center, it does have an impressive number of quality publications. In the area of company-sponsored foundations and corporate giving, Taft's publication is more thorough and on point than those of the Foundation Center. The good news is that most cooperating collections and the five Foundation Center libraries are stocked with selected Taft Group publications. Taft also has two CD-ROMs. Get on the Taft mailing list.

Another publication that I sometimes use, particularly when working with advocacy organizations, is *The Grant Seekers Guide*. This is a directory originally conceived by members of the National Network of Grantmakers. These grantmakers are committed to social and economic justice. Their publication is designed with the smaller, less-established organization in mind.

A final publication is *The Chronicle of Philanthropy*. In each edition, this bimonthly publication presents several condensed annual foundation reports and information about recent grant awards. The Chronicle has a web site and a program on computer disk, or CD-ROM, that enables searches for foundation sources.

There are many other national sources of information about foundations, but the ones given here I have found to be the best and most reliable. Specific information on how to avail yourself of all the references mentioned in this chapter can be found in "VC's Recommended Resources."

States also have directories of foundations. Some are good and others not so good. Most cooperating collections will have the directory for their state. Those published by donor groups such as The Donors Forum in Chicago, The Michigan Council of Foundations, and The Indiana Donor Alliance are excellent. Also, many not-for-profit management support groups, such as The Texas Center for Nonprofit Resources, have excellent, accurate publications, and they are generally inexpensive.

Although there is a great deal of free assistance available, your agency should invest effort, time, *and* money on research. To glean information about an agency's commitment and preparedness for securing foundation funding, I usually ask its program developers and proposal writers a very simple question: How much money has your agency made available for research materials and activities? If the answer is none, the agency's success at securing foundation funding may be in jeopardy. An agency's commitment to research is also determined by the time it allows its procurement staff to work on this activity. It is unsound management to overburden the person(s) who writes proposals with other responsibilities.

Allocating money for research is a sticky point with many small, community-based organizations with which I have worked. This is usually because they are under-funded as it is and have to make tough decisions when it comes to allocating their funds. This is a reality, so to a certain degree I understand it and quite often try to work with them on brainstorming some ways they can generate funds just for this area. What I have a harder time comprehending, though, is larger, more traditional organizations not wanting to spend money on research materials. Oftentimes, many of them have discretionary monies that haven't been allocated for other needs. I remind them of the capitalist manifesto: It takes money to get money. In other words, they have the money available to purchase resources that can aid them in securing more money. Then, ideally, they'll be in an even better position to address the needs of their clients and constituents.

Foundation dollars are limited, and this makes for selective funding. The more research done, the better your chances of walking away with the funding you desire. And it is only *after* the research is done that you will have an accurate list of potential funders in hand.

Information from the Foundation

The research is done and your potential funder is identified. The next step is to request information from the foundation. Call and request a copy of their annual reports, application information, newsletters, and whatever else the foundation will share. Some foundations publish newsletters and other publications that can be helpful in understanding their interests and priorities. If they have a web site, go to it to see what additional information may be available. Study all the information received, particularly the annual report. The foundation's annual report may be available at a cooperating collection, but get your own copy so you can mark on it with a highlighter or make notes. Be clear on the foundation's mission and interests. They may be different from what is stated in a directory. From the information you receive directly from the foundation, always re-verify that whatever information you've gotten from a directory is accurate. Review its staff information and identify the staff member who will most likely handle your request. Who is on the foundation's board of directors? What is known about any board member that might give you a better understanding of the foundation? These things done, identify one to three grant recipients and call them. One of the best sources of information about a foundation can come from its grant recipients.

I surprise clients and workshop participants when I suggest for them to call previous grant recipients. Why would they want to help me, they say? Won't they feel we want to take money from them? Won't they see us as competitors? Maybe or maybe not is the answer. Find out. Be friendly when calling. This is no time to practice your cross-examination skills. If a grant recipient is unwilling to cooperate, do not push. A person who hoards and who thinks we are in the middle of famine is not going to be helpful. Find someone willing to talk, and you can then establish rapport by identifying the common cause. Congratulate them on their accomplishment of having been awarded a grant. Following are some questions to ask:

1. Was this the first time your agency submitted this program request to the foundation?
2. Has your agency previously received funding from this foundation?
3. Who was your contact at the foundation? You should have a good idea if you reviewed the annual report. Ask for information that will help you work with this person? (Check to see if this individual is listed in biographical books like *Who's Who*)
4. Was there a meeting with someone at the foundation before submitting the proposal? Was there some other kind of contact with the foundation? Did these contacts play a role in helping develop your program?
5. What is the foundation's process for determining grant awards?
6. How long did it take for your grant to be awarded?

Other questions will also come to mind. Ask to see their proposal. Occasionally, a grantee will send a copy of their proposal. If they initially say no, ask for a copy without the budget. Treat this document only as a proposal funded by your projected source, not as a model.

Public Funds

Researching government sources is similar to researching foundations. Again, the more data gathered, the easier it is to prepare your proposal. When applying to a governmental agency in charge of disbursing newly authorized program funds, get a copy of the law authorizing the appropriation. After reviewing the legislation and any extraneous documents associated with it, such as conference reports and subsequent public laws, you will have additional insight into the intent of the legislation, and this will be helpful in preparing your proposal.

The most accessible federal dollars in our multilevel system of government are available through local and state agencies. This is so because the main way the federal government disburses money for projects is through block grants to state agencies. This distribution process separates the federal government's mission of being responsible primarily for demonstration programs, research, and the transfer of technology from that of state governments, which is the responsibility of providing direct services. Funds for services come from federal block grants. Petition a state agency for these funds. The 104th and 105th Congresses lifted most of the regulations that previously guided disbursement of these grants, but state agencies now must negotiate accountability and performance outcomes with their federal grantors. This requirement gets to the crux of why the evaluation component of proposals is so key. Spend some time on understanding the inner-workings of your state agencies. For example, if your organization is dedicated to substance abuse prevention, establish a relationship with your city, county, or regional substance abuse agency. Try to understand where its funds come from and how it operates. Know how the individuals who work there make decisions and award grants. If there is an advisory board, familiarize yourself with the members and attend meetings to get a feel for the group's dynamics. Identify the most appropriate person to talk with and do so regularly.

Also do these things with your state agency that is responsible for substance abuse prevention. Not only will this agency be responsible for federal block grant funds, but it will also administer any substance abuse funds allocated by the state. The objective is to stay informed about agency priorities and funding opportunities. Obtain a copy of the state plan and all other available publications. It will not hurt to make a couple trips a year to the state capital to meet with agency personnel.

Forge relationships with individuals from more than just one agency. Find out what other

agencies the substance abuse prevention agency coordinates with and learn about their operations also. The state's criminal justice department might communicate with the substance abuse prevention agency. Funds from a criminal justice block grant may be available to support programs that are of interest to your organization. Do the same thing at the federal level. Do not let distance be a barrier to communication with the federal agency responsible for substance abuse prevention.
Review their publications and all research they have funded. Try to develop a relationship with some individual in the agency. These activities will help you stay informed of the priorities of each agency and to understand their relationships with your clients. Technology can be very helpful in learning information about public funding. Lots of information about this subject is available online. Keep in mind that having access to information through the Internet should not replace personal contact. John Nasbitt, author of *Mega Trends,* writes about "high touch." In this best selling book, he points out that "high tech" and "high touch" go hand in hand. The more society is bombarded with artificial intelligence and has to acquire goods and services through computers and other machines, the more people have a need for personal contact with other people. According to Nasbitt, such practical and convenient activities as teleconferencing will never replace face-to-face meetings entirely because "...People want to go to

the office. People want to be with other people."
This is useful information for those of you who rely
on computers for doing research. You'd do well to
balance that out with also gathering information
directly from people. These may be some of the
same people who have influence or make decisions
about grant awards. High-touch relationships and
high-tech information are both essential to grant
solicitation.

Political Consideration

To discuss fund solicitation and not discuss the
part politics plays in this process would be remiss.
Organizations should maintain contact with their
elected officials--city and county representatives,
state representatives and state senators, and US
Congresspersons. Get these individuals involved
with your efforts, but do not involve yourself with
partisan politics. There is no need to pass out
leaflets or to canvass for a candidate unless it is for
personal reasons. If you do, separate this activity
from your agency and its mission. Not-for-profits
need not involve themselves in partisan politics.
Besides the legal implications of such activity,
what happens to your agency when your chosen
party loses?

Meet with staff of your congressional and state
representatives. Do this even if contact has
previously been made with the elected official.
Connecting with a staff person is essential to

maintaining a relationship with an elected official because a staff person can be more easily reached when the politician is unavailable. When meeting, refer to your clients as *their* constituents. Let them know about the scope of services your organization is providing *their* constituents and how *their* constituents are benefiting from your agency's work. Explain your needs and ask for assistance with your efforts to secure funds. Specifically, ask for assistance in soliciting public funds to continue serving their constituents. Elected officials' staff members may be able to contact appropriate agencies on your behalf and set up meetings.

Know on what committees your representative serves. If she shows interest in the subject of your project or sits on a committee connected to an agency that your organization plans to contact, ask for her opinion. Offer the expertise of your agency to your representative's staff and committee. Let her know the areas in which your agency can be most helpful. For example, a health provider to older individuals could offer to help review a bill the representative is sponsoring that affects senior citizens. Do not confuse these activities with lobbying. It is not lobbying until elected officials are told specifically how you want them to vote on legislation. Let your representatives know that your agency personnel is available to participate in hearings they or their legislative colleagues might conduct. Offer to facilitate or hold public forums they may conduct for constituent communities. Of course, the forum should be related to your agency's mission. Remember, no partisan events or activities!

Make your elected official a partner on your team. When writing the proposal and soliciting letters of support, get one from your representative showing his/her involvement with your project. Individuals and organizations I have worked with regularly receive letters from their elected officials. These letters generally say nothing unless time has been given to keep representatives informed and involved with your cause. Then those letters clearly show their interest in your program and their constituents' need for it.

Some Additional Resources

There are many resources that can be helpful in tracking public funds, particularly federal and block grant funds. The *Catalog of Federal Domestic Assistance* is one. It is a government-wide compendium of federal programs, projects, services, and activities that provide assistance or benefits to the public. *The Catalog* is a necessity when tracking financial or non-financial programs. It has good instructions and is easy to use. It is also available on CD-ROM, disk, and on-line, and it covers more than just grants. It is an excellent resource and is useful in identifying a broad range of available assistance.

Order a copy of the *United States Government Manual*. As the official handbook of the federal government, this publication provides comprehensive information on the agencies of the legislative, judicial, and executive branches. It includes information on quasi-official agencies; international organizations in which the United States participates; and a variety of boards, commissions, and committees.

The Federal Register is issued each federal working day. It is the system for publishing Presidential and regulatory documents as well as proposed rules and notices, including grant announcements. Notices of newly authorized and funded programs will be of greatest interest. As useful as this publication is, I don't recommend that you subscribe to it, because is tedious reading. It is available online and at public and federal depository libraries. There are ways to use *The Federal Register* without reading it every day. For example, do what I do: subscribe to newsletters that publish excerpts, or access information from it on various web sites, including The Grantsmanship Center's. There may be times when the information provided by secondary sources is not thorough enough for your needs, and you will need to examine the official document itself. So do what I do, go to the library. There you can go online and download it or make a copy of any part of the publication you want; it's not copyrighted.

The Government Printing Office distributes, free of charge, printed and electronic publications to approximately fourteen hundred depository libraries nationwide. (Get a listing from the Superintendent of Documents.) Read about depository libraries in the *Catalog of Federal Domestic Assistance* and the *U.S. Government Manual*. Depository libraries are a resource most program developers and proposal writers need to be aware of and use.

The Federal Assistance Monitor is a newsletter published twice monthly by CD Publications. It gives a comprehensive picture of federal funding announcements, private grants, rule changes, and legislative actions affecting all community programs. CD Publications offers news in specific program areas. *Substance Abuse Funding News* is one of their publications that I find quite useful.

Capitol Publications publishes *Federal Grants and Contracts Weekly*. This newsletter reviews available federal grants and contracts. There is also a monthly supplement on foundation funding and updates on legislation and trends.

Again, I recommend one of The Grantsmanship Center's publications: *Basic Grantsmanship Center Library*. This publication lists some of the best resource materials available.

The Chronicle of Philanthropy puts out a comprehensive resource list of publications and services each January. Obtaining back issues from the publisher is possible.

Online Resources

The number of online resources is growing and having a positive effect on the search for private and federal funding sources. There are many online sources where information on federal, state, and private philanthropic organizations is available. Most research on public funding can now be done on the Internet. Private foundations have not caught up with the government in this area, but are rapidly improving. I will talk more about this in the next chapter, "Cyberspace."

In "VC's Recommended Resources" I have included quite a few additional publications and resources that are also helpful in fund solicitation.

So what this all boils down to is when it comes to finding a funding source, the information is out there, and there are several avenues for obtaining it. You just have to make the connection. And whether you are seeking to connect to an individual, an agency, or information, you have to do the research that is required. Sure this is a time-consuming task, but its one that will dramatically increase your group's chances of getting funded. And keep in mind, when steadily gathering information about any subject, the accumulative learning factor kicks in. You become more familiar with the sources and what is happening in the field, so you find yourself not having to read materials quite as completely. In essence, as with most things, the more frequently you research, the easier the task becomes.

Stalking the Elusive Dollars in Cyberspace

"You know what? I'm getting tired of hearing about the Internet." So said the cynical man in one of the many television commercials extolling the Internet.

Well, tired or not, the Internet is here with us, and it has woven its way into all facets of our lives. This is true for even those who are so far removed from computers that they only know one kind of mouse--a furry four-legged rodent that likes cheese. How so? Because the concerns that most control, design, and influence our lives all rely on information and communication received through the Internet. These concerns include our armed forces, commercial organizations, educational institutions, government bodies, healthcare providers, financial institutions, and legal justice bodies. To a lesser, but growing, extent, our religious, family, cultural, and social groups are also connected to the Net. And these broad groupings that I have identified don't even begin to fully characterize the complexity of the various groups spreading their opinions and information over this massive network.

It was not until the latter stages of writing this book that I decided to include a chapter on computer technology or, more specifically, the Internet. But the more I relied on it myself, the more I realized any book that is written for the purpose of informing its readers of informational sources *requires* including information about the Internet. The Net cannot be ignored. This technology is changing the way we communicate, access information, conduct business, and entertain ourselves. It has changed the way organizations develop programs, identify funding sources, and write proposals. However, even though it is changing how we communicate, Robin Zeff makes an important point in her book *The Nonprofit Guide to the Internet*. She says, "The Internet poses no threat to traditional communication processes, but rather it expands them beyond time and space, physical and geographical barriers and social economic standards that are the present determinants of most communication."

Most organizations and businesses are already using some aspect of computer technology in their work. At the very minimum, there are fax machines and word processing software. How could proposal writers get along without these tools? Some have taken the next step and gone online. This technology is being used to discover, explore and discuss program ideas, gather program information, and form collaborative relationships. And more now are even accessing information about funding opportunities.

Just What Is The Internet?

The Internet is a global electronic network of computers made up of government, industry, academic, and research sectors. It started in 1969 at the University of California, Los Angeles, as a program to link computers for defense research. Relaxed restrictions on Internet access by the federal government in 1990 led to public interest and broader use. No one manages this large complex system. The various networks, access providers, and users of the Internet dictate the policies, user behavior, and most administrative matters.

The Internet has become a vast and populous communication medium with millions of regular users world wide. How vast? I've heard some estimates of 20 million and others as high as 50 million. In truth, nobody really knows because the number of people accessing the Net is growing too rapidly to keep an accurate tally. But what we do know is that any kind of information an individual is curious about or wishes to circulate or publish is somewhere on the World Wide Web.

For clarification, most people use the terms "Internet" and "World Wide Web" synonymously; however, they are not one in the same. Instead, they work in conjunction with each other. Since discussion of the Internet here is to aid readers in proposal writing and program planning, and knowing the distinction between the two does not further that cause, I will not take the time to expound on it. However, if you are curious about the differentiation, check out a computer book, or, better yet, do a search online.

Having unrestricted access to information on the Internet does have its share of woe sayers, mainly those who seek to protect children and control the appropriateness of information that is distributed. But it also has its share of supporters, two of the most prominent of which are President Clinton and Vice-President Gore, both of whom participated in NetDay 96. This was a one-day effort by volunteers to wire computers in California schools for access to the Internet. NetDay attracted 20,000 volunteers with the goal of wiring 20 percent of California's 13,000 schools. Additionally, during the 1996 Presidential Campaign, President Clinton stressed the idea of connecting every school classroom in the country to the Internet.

What Does All This Mean to Proposal Writers
and Program Planners?

The Internet intimidates many users and would-be users. Many people are discouraged from accessing the system and its benefits because of its complexity. This includes--but is not limited to-- many program planners and proposal writers as well as other staff members of not-for-profit organizations. Although, because of competitive elements in the marketplace and advancing technology, the Net is relatively "user friendly." And, generally, when using the Internet, people do not make irreparable mistakes. Usually the worst that happens is they get separated from a source of information that they found helpful because they were lured to even more exciting or stimulating web sites. And even with this mishap, the browsers (software that enables you to move from site to site on the Net) provide easy techniques to minimize it from happening.

What follows are descriptions of some common Internet tools, services and features that provide alternatives for getting information and for getting online.

Electronic mail (E-mail) allows anyone with a networked computer to send a message to anyone else connected to the Internet. This is an extremely cost-efficient way to communicate with others in different telephone billing zones. Other options are mailing lists and discussion groups for people with common interests. These services travel along the same electronic lines as E-mail.

Bulletin Board Services. Bulletin boards exist independent of the Internet. They are devoted to a specific topic or organization, and information about such is posted in a central place. There are thousands of bulletin board services locally, nationally, and internationally. Some include a relatively closed network. However, others offer opportunities to reach millions. Users can get news, download files of information, receive technical support, and discuss a multitude of subjects.

I should point out that besides providing their own information and services, many bulletin boards provide limited access to the Internet.

Commercial Networks and Internet Service Providers. Other than accommodating their subscribers with access to the Internet, commercial networks such as America On Line (AOL), CompuServe, and the Microsoft Network (MSN) provide e-mail access to user forums, public domain software, and other pertinent information. There are also many network services that specifically target not-for-profits: HandsNet, for example, provides e-mail, news information forums, and other resources for human service and public interest organizations.

You can also access the Net through thousands of local access providers offering this service. These small Internet Service Providers (ISPs)--unlike AOL, CompuServe, and MSN--do not provide news, stock updates, or the original content of news stories. They are merely an entree into the World Wide Web and its cornucopia of information. Such providers are rapidly springing up nationwide.

Another thing that often comes with ISP service is a small amount of megabytes of space on the Net, which you can use to publish a web page. This is a feature that can be useful if your agency wants to spotlight itself or some of the activities its involved with. To take advantage of this space, it is not necessary to have a domain name (definition will follow) as it is if you are trying to display an independent web site on the Net.

Some users view the large commercial networks as "Internet training wheels." America Online, CompuServe, and MSN are more expensive, but they are also easier to use. A beginner might be better off with one of the large providers. Once familiar with the Internet, switch to a less costly ISP.

Community Networks. Developed around local, state or regional geographic areas, community networks, such as freenets, provide free access to e-mail and information sources to members of the community, including government and not-for-profit agencies.

Electronic Databases, such as Lexis/Nexus, Dialog, and Dow Jones, offer information for a fee. Unlike the networks, there is no communication or networking between users. Users simply download the information. For example, the Foundation Center's *Foundation Directory* and *Grant Index* are on Dialog.

Uniform Resource Locator (URL). This is the standard form for giving an address for any web site on the World Wide Web. To be more specific, it is also the actual combination of words, letters, numbers, and figures that must be entered in the computer when trying to access a web site. Having this information and entering it into the computer to take you to a specific web site is synonymous with giving a cab driver a specific street name and number so she can drive you to a specific location in a city.

Web Site. This is a site on the Net that contains at least one page of information--and most often more. A home page is the first page to a web site, and from there you can jump to the site's subsequent pages. Usually information on these subsequent pages is more detailed about a specific subject or item. Information on web sites is conveyed through the use of different mediums:

text, graphics, sound, and often even video. The site may also have links (connection tools) that make it easy for you to travel from it to other relevant sites. The information presented on web sites can frequently be printed or downloaded to your own computer. Also, because web sites are controlled by the individual entities that publish them, information posted on them and their designs can, and do, change regularly. The development of web pages has become easier, so often using community college students or do-it-yourself software can be a very cost-effective way for getting this done.

Domain Name. This is a name you can create and use to reflect your agency's presence on the Web. It is like a title that represents your service or organization. Again, to use a real world example, it is like the name of a building that distinguishes it from other buildings in a city. Domain names cost $100 and have to be re-registered every two years. They are issued by Inter/NIC Registration Services. Under a domain name, you can publish your own web site. This is an idea worth checking into because it can be a very practical way to get your agency or program more exposure, and can be especially useful in a publicity campaign or for fundraising efforts.

This list only scratches the surface. It has been included strictly for introducing a few basic Internet features and services. The easiest way for most people to familiarize themselves with the Net is to just dive in and start surfing. All ISPs and Internet browsers come with tutorials that provide descriptions of the technical terms associated with Internet use. They also give instructions on how to navigate the Net and conduct searches for specific information. These instructions tend to be basic, but when learning about the Internet, basic is better because then there's less chance of you getting overwhelmed by its vast features. You could probably surf the Net every day and never stop discovering new information about its makeup, use, and features.

Using Online Technology for Program Planning and Proposal Writing

Use of the Internet goes beyond looking for requests for proposals or finding or researching funding sources. It can be a useful tool in all facets of program planning and proposal writing. Some individuals and organizations I work with believe going online is primarily for identifying sources of money. I find this to be only partially true. Information about public funding, particularly from the federal government, can be found, but when it comes to researching foundations, online is not the best place to look. The federal government has a wealth of information on the web. All federal agencies have a web site. Also, many federal publications are online. Most federal agencies distribute requests for proposals or applications by the web. In addition to the agencies' sites, there are some excellent indexes of government funding sources, such as the Federal Information Exchange. Again, though, when it comes to foundations, your best bet is still using print media like the ***Foundation Directory*** and ***Foundation Reporter***. Both of these publications are also on CD-ROMS.

Although, finding information online about foundations does continue to get easier--faster than I thought it would. A number of foundations have developed excellent web sites; however, only a few of them include essential information regarding previous grant awards. I think David Lamb, director of Donor Acknowledgement and Prospect Research at the University of Washington, sums up the situation best in ***The Grantseeker's Handbook of Essential Internet Sites**** when he says, "But in comparison to the total number of charitable organizations in the world, the percentage of corporations and foundations that have created useful web sites with good grant data rounds to zero."

Here are some ways I think the Internet can be helpful in the whole fund solicitation process:

1. Identifying varied funding opportunities, particularly federal and state funds;

2. Obtaining examples of effective programs;
3. Discussing problems and getting quick and informed assistance from others in the field;
4. Finding hard data to document problems and data to support program approaches;
5. Promoting your program and establishing collaborative efforts;
6. Soliciting contributions (cyber fundraising) or selling merchandise: a product on a home page.

The Internet can bring a prospective funding source to your fingertips, but it cannot write a proposal or tell everything there is to know about that source (at least not right now). A well-written proposal containing solid data that addresses a problem is the only thing that has a reasonable chance of capturing a funding source. The Internet is not a magic solution for getting money now or in the future. This technology is a tool that merely helps in gathering and processing astonishing amounts of information, but such information is meaningless if you lack the ability to plan a program and write a proposal that expresses your agency's effectiveness.

Even though the Internet is advancing rapidly, it is still new to most program planners and proposal writers. In an informal survey I have been conducting over the last few years, I ask each of the participants in The Grantsmanship Center classes I conduct how many of them are using online technology. Surprisingly, the numbers are still small. As recently as 1998, in an average class of 25 participants, no more than 10 or 11 answer affirmatively. What I find even more surprising is that the majority of the time participants say they use their own personal sources when going online.

More not-for-profits are becoming interested in going online, and in most instances I am a staunch supporter of this decision. However, acquiring the resources--an up-to-date computer and software, at least one extra telephone line, funds to pay an ISP, etc.--does cost, so do some homework and planning before expending or committing any funds for Internet access. Weigh the potential benefits against the fiscal and operational drawbacks that online technology could have for your agency.

One other less costly way to access the World Wide Web is by using a computer at a public library or buying computer time by the hour at a Kinko's or some other office service store.

Taking into account these cautions, I predict that not-for profit agencies in the next two years will have to use online technology to solicit grants and develop successful programs. All aspects of the proposal and grant process will be affected by this technology. There is already a wealth of program development information from online government sources.

Federal, state, and local government sources have set up resource centers, clearinghouses, and online bulletin boards with information on research studies, model programs, grant andevaluation procedures, etc. I work with many alcohol tobacco and drug prevention programs and use the *Prevline*, which is maintained by the Center for Substance Abuse. In my state, California, the substance abuse authority sponsors *Prevnet*. This resource provides research articles, funding information, and program updates. Most states I work in have a similar system. For example, the Indiana Prevention Resource Center at Indiana University maintains a web site. There are many more online sites to explore. Start with your state. After finding out what is available in your state, move on to federal sources.

More than 350 foundations have sites that allow individuals from around the world to obtain information about their goals, accomplishments, and programs. When I began writing this book, only a few of the over 38,000 foundations in the United States had a presence on the Internet. By the time you read this, more foundations will be online.

Some foundations with web sites post their e-mail addresses. Bell South Foundation in Atlanta, the Charles A. Dana Foundation in New York, and others have electronic application forms that grantseekers can fill out. This is a growing trend. Some grantseekers are impatient that more foundations have not followed this move, but foundation staff are reluctant to becoming too accessible, especially to large numbers of inappropriate requests. One way that some are handling this situation is by developing sites for one-way communication and not listing the e-mail addresses of staff members. They give only the postal address and telephone number of the foundation.

Related to this issue, Jody Curtis, editor of *Foundation News and Commentary*, reported on 21 foundation executives interviewed by the Foundation Center who by using computers are looking to streamline their proposal review process in the future. However, all reported that *at the present time* they prefer to have proposals mailed to them, and none reported accepting proposals electronically or on disk.

The Foundation Center and the Council on Foundations both maintain sites for online research. The Grantsmanship Center web site gives a "Tip of the Day," regularly updates information from the *Federal Register* and other publications, and has a link to the *Catalog of Federal Domestic Assistance.* From these sites, you can get help with accessing public and private sources. (See VC's recommended resources.)

Besides using the Internet for identifying resources and funding sources, it can also be useful when actually writing the proposal. Going online can eliminate the use of out-dated statistical quotations and can cut unsupported assumptions from your work. Recently, I was working on a proposal with a man who was responsible for developing and writing the problem statement. My quick review of the statement showed it contained several unsupported assumptions about a low-income target group and their access to healthcare. The statements were true, but he needed citations or quotes from credible sources to support their validity. Unfortunately, it was 10:00 p.m., and we were working against a fast-approaching deadline. I called upon my colleague Ed Sanchez, who is quite proficient at using the Net as a research tool. After twenty minutes of searching, he was able to retrieve citations and quotations my fellow proposal writer needed for making his problem statement more solid. Traditionally when developing the problem statement, proposal writers have gathered information from libraries, research centers, conferences, magazine articles, seminars and colleagues, but as demonstrated in this scenario, information can frequently be found quicker and more conveniently online. Just like convenience stores, the Internet is available 24-hours a day, seven days a week, and all holidays. Funding sources are requesting more information because they know the data is easily available.

If your agency has this technology, learn to use it! You will become a more efficient and effective program planner, and that is good for your agency. A more personal reason for becoming proficient at using the Internet is because program planning with a not-for-profit does not traditionally offer lifetime job security, especially if your salary is paid from a grant. You will be the first laid off when financial cuts have to be made. However, your mastery of Internet technology is transferable to other jobs, and that is good for you.

Initially, I did find Internet technology intimidating, but I learned quickly. Right now you have a choice to use it or not. I expect that with the rate the Internet is being embraced, two or three years from now you'll fall short of industry standards if you do not know how to use it. In a forward written for the book **Crossing The Internet Threshold,** Clifford Lynch, director of Library Automation for the University of California, stated, "The Internet is now a place to disseminate information, to seek information, to communicate, to teach, to learn, and to conduct business and commerce. But for those not yet part of this dynamic, rapidly, growing medium, pathways across the Internet threshold have been somewhat mysterious and hard to identify. Yet, there is no substitute for being there." Do not frustrate yourself trying to keep up with everything on the large, diverse and ever-changing Internet. Nobody knows all there is to know about it. Learn what is needed to be informed and effective in your role.

Participating in training programs, workshops, and conferences are excellent ways to learn and stay informed. When selecting a training course, be sure to get some information on the level the instruction is designed for, because (as most training does) computer instruction runs the gamut from the very basic to very advanced. One advantage to participating in an Internet training class is that more than likely the instructor will be familiar with what computer hardware you will need to get up and running. Even though the cost of computers is steadily dropping, you still may be able to save more money if some knowledgeable person can inform you on how to upgrade a current system you may have. Sure, you can get this same information from talking to a salesperson, but ofentimes their intent is to sell you the latest and the best, and the latest and the best may be something you can do without.

Also, some not-for-profit support and technical assistance centers conduct low-cost workshops. As I travel around the country, I see advertisements for Internet workshops in the business section of metropolitan newspapers. Using books and other printed sources to hone your Internet skills is a viable alternative to attending a class.. Just keep in mind that because Internet technology is ever changing, many printed sources are out dated by the time they first hit bookstore shelves.

Bottom line, take advantage of instructional sources available and invest in educating yourself about the internet. It's paying dividends now, and will continue to do so in the future--for you, your agency, and your clients. Lynch points are relevant to not-for-profits. You have been forewarned; act accordingly.

*This directory, *The Grantseeker's Handbook of Essential Internet Sites,* published by Capitol Publications, is one of the most useful sources I have found on internet sites related to funding sources. It is a bit pricey, but it is well worth the cost. (See VC's Recommended Resources)

"Da Board"

In reviewing publications on proposal writing, I found little on the role of the board of directors. Not surprising, because too often boards stand outside this and other project processes. This is particularly true in human service and community-based agencies that are involved with anti-poverty programs, substance abuse prevention, mental health, or juvenile delinquency. It baffles me that many of my clients do not expect board members to be involved in fundraising. This hands-off behavior on the part of boards must be eliminated. The board should be an important part of every not-for-profit organization's grant procurement and fund development plans. An uninvolved board can hurt an agency's chances of acquiring funding, particularly with foundations.

Let us examine the board's role in soliciting grants. First, no matter who develops the program and writes the proposal, the board, by law, is ultimately responsible for securing its organization's financial resources. The financing of the organization's operations should be the greatest single concern for the not-for-profit board of directors. Peter F. Drucker (who many consider the Father of Modern Management) emphasizes this point in his book *Managing the Nonprofit Organization* when he writes:

> The board is the premier fundraising organ of the nonprofit organization, an important role it does not have in the for-profit business. If a board does not actively lead in fund development, getting the funds the organization needs may be very difficult.

Funding sources are concerned with your agency's financial development capacity and may view your board's participation as an integral part of that capability. This is an easy and quick way for them to assess a board's commitment. If 100 percent of the directors are contributing and 20 percent of the total dollars obtained from individuals is coming from the board, then the source sees a level of commitment that will allow it to invest in the organization's effort. If the board is not substantially contributing to the organization, a funding source becomes reluctant to contribute. To digress a minute, the influence structure plays on this reluctance is clear. Because even though idealistically foundations are committed to causes that not-for-profits conduct, they are still influenced by capitalistic values. This is because our capitalistic system is the structure in which they operate. (See the previous discussion on systems, chapter on Program Planning.)

I realize the idea of the board contributing to the organization can be controversial, but this is only because too many boards are uninformed about what their commitment to an organization entails. Many of my clients' board members come from low-income neighborhoods, so these clients say such board members cannot afford to make a financial contribution. Still, though, they allow such people on the board because they want their board to accurately reflect their community socially and economically. I think that these statements undermine the board's duty to financially contribute to the organization. There is no one sitting on a board who cannot afford to contribute $10 once a year to something they care about. And I find it hard to believe that most people cannot come up with $50. The directors can make special exceptions on a case-by-case basis for those genuinely unable to contribute, but this should not be an excuse for the absence of a stated policy requiring board member financial contributions.

The organization must decide contribution amounts that are fair. In some organizations, there is no minimum amount. The members give what they can, but everyone must give something. Other not-for-profits may have guidelines, but no requirements. Still, others have a minimum ranging from fifty to one thousand dollars per person. Most organizations I have worked with have set minimum levels ranging from 50 to 200 dollars. Board members should be expected to contribute financially even if they are providing other kinds of donations to the organization. Not-for-profits usually appreciate donations of needed materials, equipment, and services, so if a member can show, through adequate documentation, that she used her own personal cash to acquire or provide such things, then perhaps that can be translated into a cash contribution. But you have to be able to show on the books the cash value of such items. Volunteer assistance does not substitute for a cash contribution.

Beyond donating money, directors must help raise it. Some may feel uncomfortable personally soliciting money from individuals, but may be willing to identify potential donors, develop a mailing list, write letters, plan fundraisers, or write proposals. Ideally, every board member will take responsibility for one of these tasks.

Thomas Wolf, in his book *Managing a Nonprofit Organization,* says there are three questions funding sources want answered about an organization's board:

1. What percentage of your directors are making financial contributions to the organization?
   Answer: Should be 100 percent.

2. How much in total does the organization receive in board contributions?
Answer: Should be a substantial portion of the total contributions--perhaps 20 to 30 percent.
3. How active is the board in soliciting funds?
Answer: Should be "very active." And it should indicate that "they implement fundraising activities."

Very few organizations I work with can give positive responses to all of these questions. However, giving a positive response to each of these questions can become organizational goals. And there must be a plan to meet not only the goals, but also a plan to recruit directors who agree with them.

Also in his book, when writing on the subject of the responsibilities of boards of directors, Wolf identifies what he considers the principal areas of their responsibility. Besides fundraising there are five others. The others do not relate exclusively to fundraising, but more to assessing the overall efficiency of boards of directors. They are on point in identifying some valid expectations organizations should have of their boards of directors. Boards that function in all these areas can be characterized as fully functioning, and they are a tremendous asset to the organizations they serve. You can find these areas listed at the end of this chapter. I think you will find this information helpful, and I recommend you use it in assessing and possibly improving the efficiency of your organization's board of directors.

When selecting directors, recruiting people who have contacts with prominent citizens in the public and private sector is important. These people should be credible and have reputations for getting things done. Make sure your board has representatives from the small business sector and your target group. A well rounded board should be representative of all segments of the community that your organization is servicing.

An effective board of directors also needs to bring together people from varying backgrounds and disciplines. All racial, ethnic, economic and social groups in your target community should be represented so that the board can understand different perspectives on controversial issues. Your organization's board should be composed of people who have knowledge and expertise in the following areas:

1. Local political structure and its environs;
2. Not-for-profit leadership and their boards;
3. Organizational planning or programming related to the agency's mission.
4. Fiscal management related to not-for-profits, including legal matters such as contracts and agreements.
5. Fund development, donor solicitation, and fundraising events;

6. Marketing or public relations.
7. Personnel management.

An organization's board roster can be part of a fundraising strategy, but be careful to not create a board that has only name value or "letterhead" directors. Negligible involvement by high-profile directors will not give your organization credibility. People dedicated to your organization's mission and who are willing to work to make things happen are the kind of people needed. However, if your organization could use some window dressing, put together a blue-ribbon list as an advisory committee. An honorary chair and board may be beneficial to an agency's image. But keep in mind, this supplemental board is no substitute for a quality board that creates policy.

One of the boards I sit on has a "panel of experts." This panel, which consists of people skilled in specific areas, advises the directors. They share their expertise with our organization and are named on our letterhead. We ask each panelist to attend one organizational meeting a year. This advisory board in no way supplants the organization's board of directors that has a legal obligation to the agency. One key distinction between the two boards is the advisement board makes suggestions and recommendations, while the governing board creates policy and makes decisions.

Do not recruit only board members who work for other 50l(c)(3)s. They may have divided loyalties that favor the fundraising efforts of their employing organization over yours. The board of directors or chief executive officer of the agency that employs them may have expectations that severely hinder their efforts for your agency. One instance exemplifying this that I'm familiar with is when one agency's program proposal showed up on another agency's application to the same funder, on the same date. Often, who a board member receives a paycheck from will determine which organization he/she will be most loyal to. No way am I saying *anyone* who works for another 501(c)(3) should not be considered for being on your organization's board. But I'm saying because loyalties are often tested, it would be unwise to have your complete board consisting of such individuals.

A board of directors needs to establish a philosophy to guide them in their fund solicitation efforts. This philosophy should address such concerns as: Do board members have objections to earning funds either through fee-for-service work or other entrepreneurial efforts? Should the agency's clients' fundraising values be considered;

do they care where the money comes from as long as the problem is addressed? Are there any donors in particular that should be avoided? I have worked with organizations that will not solicit or accept funds from a certain sector. (Remember Dr. Edna Martin, one of my early-on mentors?) Some of my clients in the drug and alcohol prevention field will not accept funds from the alcohol beverage industry. A few years ago when South Africa was under apartheid rule, some clients would not accept funds from any organization that invested in or had holdings in that country. Philosophical values should not be assumed. They must be explored and given due consideration when forming the philosophy. If not, they can lead to tensions among board members that can undermine successful funding efforts. A philosophy should address the following:

1. Things the board members are willing to do to raise funds;
2. Their attitudes toward raising money;
3. Their preferences for or against seeking government funds;
4. Their position on being for or against seeking business funding;
5. Their willingness or unwillingness to charge fees for services;

6. Their willingness or unwillingness to participate in entrepreneurial efforts;
7. How their planning and goal setting will support the organization's mission.

The staff should also take part in developing the philosophy, but it is not their mission exclusively. In my experience, staff often are too close to the situation to be objective. They let their biases and other interests--like a pay check--get in the way. The board should oversee development of this philosophy and should revisit it from time to time, particularly after a board election. New directors may have different views and the philosophy may take some fine tuning.

A philosophy exists even if it is not stated. Each director has his own ideas, but it is important that the board have a clear group philosophy that addresses planning, goal setting, and support for the organization's mission. I have worked with boards that have encouraged staff to go for *all* available grants. The board's attitude was to get funds first and decide what to do with them later.

Although it may be unwritten, this is a philosophy--albeit an inappropriate, unworkable one. A board is responsible for raising funds, but its overall reason for being is to serve the client and fulfill the organization's mission.

The Importance of Unrestricted Funds

As a former chief executive officer and board member, I know that all dollars received by a not-for-profit agency are not equal. Some are given generally to cover basic administrative costs and costs associated with any purpose that is consistent with the organization's mission. These funds are called unrestricted because the source has not obligated them to any specific programming. Obviously, the most valuable money is that which is unrestricted.

Unrestricted funds pay for non-program staff salaries as well as office space, utility bills, telephone service, and miscellaneous office costs not covered by program funds. These funds can also pay for the cost of fund development activities, which is something public source restricted funds cannot do. Organizations that depend exclusively on restricted funds find it difficult to cover basic operating expenses. Finding unrestricted funds is a constant struggle because funding sources want to pay for projects and programs. This is the primary reason the board needs a fund development plan that identifies sources of unrestricted support, and another reason why an agency needs the financial support of individuals-- who are the greatest source of unrestricted income.

Some not-for-profit organizations are in jeopardy and do not know it because their restricted funds are making them look financially sound. This problem can be addressed with an increase in unrestricted contributions. That brings us back to the board's role in fund development. The board must accept the responsibility for the collection of adequate unrestricted funds.

Some Helpful Hints

Helping a board to understand its role in fund development can be difficult. Some boards do a magnificent job of making it clear that they have no intention of getting involved in fund development. I have heard board members say "That's what we pay the executive director to do." Working with a board that has this type of attitude is hard, but the following suggestions should be helpful in readjusting their attitude in this matter.

First, train your board, formally or informally; give them written material and technical consultation. Find out what the board does not know about unrestricted and restricted funds, then develop a plan to teach them what they do not know. Where does anyone go to get educated in the ways of board members? A weekend retreat is the ideal way to do this, but it can also be done over a period of several weeks or months with written materials and discussions at the board meetings. To pull this off, the organization's leadership, particularly the executive director and the chair, will have to work together.

Second, review the bylaws and make sure they include information on the board's role in fund development. It is the board's responsibility to see that the bylaws clearly state this.

Third, evaluate the performance of the executive director and the board. Periodically the board needs to evaluate its own performance so that the agency's leadership can better understand the board's attitude about fund development and examine their efforts in this area. This evaluation will also give an indication how effectively the executive director and board are accomplishing their outcomes. Ultimately this evaluation will assess the board's fund development plan.

Fourth, if there is no fund development plan, create one. For those who are executive directors, your job demands overseeing fundraising activities. You may develop and set up a plan, but the board should sign off on it. A fund development plan gives the board ownership in the process as well as prevents you from being a solo act.

Fifth, you should work with the nominating committee. This committee is the key to the creation of a well-rounded board of directors. It should develop the criteria for the selection of board members. Keep the nominating committee updated on the agency's fund development needs.

This makes it easier for them to select board members that may be able to best further the agency's needs. For example, if a corporate strategist on the board would be helpful to the agency, tell the nominating committee.

Finally, challenge your board members if they persistently choose not to fundraise. Challenge them to find documentation that the board is not responsible for fund development. They will not find one credible source that says fundraising is not a responsibility of the board. They can delegate it, but they cannot abdicate it.

Do these suggestions work? The answer is yes! I have seen many boards change. Is it easy? No! Does it take time? You bet. It can take as long as two or three years. Conversely, the board from hell can make an organization waste scarce dollars, hurt staff, neglect clients, and even forsake its mission.

At the beginning of this chapter, I said I had seen very little about the role of the board in proposal writing books. Here I have clarified the role of the board and shed light on the issue of board governance and fund development, and the director's involvement with them in organizational funding. A board working with a solid fund development plan and in concert with the executive director can lead the organization to accomplish its mission. Developing the appropriate financial resources to meet an organization's mission is the most important activity of a board of directors.

Six Principal Areas of Responsibility for Boards of Directors
(Taken from *Managing a Nonprofit Organization,* by Thomas Wolf)

1. Determine the organization's mission and set policies for its operation, ensuring that the provisions of the organization's charter and the law are being followed;
2. Set the organization's overall program from year to year and engage in long range planning to establish its general course for the future;
3. Establish fiscal policy and boundaries, with budgets and financial controls;
4. Provide adequate resources for the activities of the organization through direct financial contributions and a commitment to fundraising;
5. Select, evaluate, and, if necessary, terminate the appointment of the chief executive;

6. Develop and maintain a communication link with the community, promoting the work of the organization.

Now What?

In this final chapter, I will summarize key points that are important for every proposal writer and program planner and program developer.

    1. **Continue to learn about writing.** Good writing is an essential ingredient of good proposals. It is not enough that you were a good writer in high school or college. Being current with *today's* language usage and writing techniques is important. Practice writing when not under an application deadline, such as when writing business letters or memoranda.

    Read books on technical writing or take a technical or business writing course. Read articles on writing in newspapers and magazines. Get in the habit of examining how magazine and newspaper articles are written. Volunteer to edit for your friends and colleagues.

    2. **Stay abreast of trends in the field in which you work.** Those who write proposals should work closely with their clients to get a current assessment of the issues and problems their communities are confronted with. Keep a file

of newspaper and magazine clippings about developments in areas you usually help plan in. If you hear about major changes in the areas you work in, then stay tuned to news programs such as **Dateline NBC** or **60 Minutes,** and from news and public information networks such as C-SPAN and CNN. This is a good way to keep a current list of credible sources.

3. Have the tools to do the job. The basic tools are phone, fax, photocopier, a good dictionary, thesaurus, and style writing manual. It also does not hurt to have an almanac or desk encyclopedia. Your computer should have a good word processing program and software that can create graphics and charts.

Access to the Internet is important. Having this technology will keep you competitive. If a computer is not available at your home or work, try the public library. Increasingly public libraries are making the Internet accessible to everyone.

4. Participate in the program planning and development process. This is especially important for those who work as freelance proposal writers. A really good proposal cannot be written unless there is participation in or observation of planning activities.

5. Improve your program planning and development skills.
Read books on needs assessment, program development, and evaluation. Take a course on program development and planning at a resource

center or local college or university. The Foundation Center and Indiana University Center for Philanthropy, and others, offer instructional programs that run from one to five days. I recommend the programs offered by the original, The Grantsmanship Center. Since 1972, The Center has trained more than 40,000 people from every state, territory, Canada, Mexico, and the United Kingdom.

Program planners and developers must know how to facilitate groups, analyze situations, negotiate or resolve conflict, and conduct needs assessments. All these skills have a role in program development and planning.

6. Maintain a good Rolodex and use your network. Good proposal writers and program developers do not operate in a vacuum. Work to expand your network and maintain it by regularly communicating with your professional contacts. Good networking is useful in acquiring needed information and in helping you to evaluate it. It also facilitates exploring program strategies and ideas with colleague. Putting out a newsletter is a convenient way to do this.

7. Use collaborative relationships. Oftentimes, it is not possible for a single agency to produce the money, facilities, staff, or other resources to carry out a program. However, a problem still needs to be addressed, and funders have indicated a willingness to fund a program that can address it. Collaboration with another organization or agency may be the solution. Use it. Some of the skills mentioned under number five are necessary for developing successful collaborative relationships.

8. Use a team effort. Program planning or proposal writing is too complex for one person. Be the lead person, or be responsible for an activity, but make sure the organization or agency for which you're working has committed the efforts of others to assist you. A process should also be laid out for what needs to be done, when, and by whom.

9. Have a good support system. Proposal writing can be frustrating. Sometimes, no matter how needed and sound your program; how well written your proposal, it does not get funded. When that happens, talk with people who understand. Call on your family or close friends, call on colleagues or other proposal writers with whom you have supportive relationships. Not only can they help dry your tears, but they can help you keep your defeats in perspective.

SO, ON YOUR WAY

In these nine chapters I've given you the blueprint and tools for writing proposals and building programs. All of the techniques, strategies, and resources have been tested and proven to work. However, keep in mind that proposal writing is a very competitive process, and in competitions not everybody wins--at least not all the time. Despite your skills and knowledge, there will always be uncontrollable variables that stand in the way of your getting funded. But don't let your defeats stop you; think of proposal writing and program planning as an ongoing effort on your part, not a one-shot trial. To do this, you must remain optimistic. Being optimistic won't just help you deal with the agony of defeat, but, according to Martin E.P. Seigman, a teacher of psychology at the University of Pennsylvania, people most likely to succeed are those who combine, "...reasonable talent with the ability to keep going in the face of defeat." The clients of not-for-profits need your expertise. Stay optimistic and be a winner: for them and for yourself.

VC's Recommended Resources

Throughout this book, I have emphasized the importance of proposal writers continuing to develop their skills and expanding their resource base. And I have mentioned many resources for doing this, the foremost of which is the Internet. I have also covered the usefulness of Foundation Center Libraries and their over 200 cooperating collections and what I see as the federal counterpart to these libraries, Federal Depository Libraries. They are the best source for finding all of the federal government publications that have been mentioned herein. An ideal situation is to have access to a library that is both a Foundation Center Cooperating Collection and a Federal Depository Library. One particular library meeting this criteria is the Boise, Idaho Public Library, and I think its Funding Information Center, under the direction of Mary K. Jones Aucutt, is the best in the country. I spent a few days in Boise consulting with Mary K. regarding this section of *The Proposal Writer's Workshop*.

Some other cooperating collections that I have found to be among the best are The Donor's Forum of Chicago, The Free Library of Philadelphia; Hogg Foundation for Mental Health, Austin Texas; Nonprofit Resource Center of Texas, San Antonio; Marquette University, Milwaukee, Wisconsin; Michigan State University, Lansing; University of Wisconsin-Madison; and the San Diego Foundation. I consider them to be among the best not only because of the materials they have available, but also because they have knowledgeable, helpful staff people that run them. I find it unfortunate that not enough cities have libraries with sufficient reference materials related to grant procurement.. And if they have the library, the staff people working there may not be as informed or helpful as need be. If this is the situation in your area, I suggest you encourage your library or some nonprofit technical assistance organization to do more about making available information pertaining to funding. All of the libraries I have mentioned are good models of effective sources. I know of several instances where only a few committed individuals served as the catalyst in their community for expanding their libraries' resources in this area.

Other than emphasizing the value of research libraries and stressing the need for more of them, also in this section I want to acquaint you with some other relevant resources that pertain to various aspects of program planning, proposal writing, and identifying potential funding sources. Additionally, some of these resources will help you with board development issues. This compilation is not all inclusive, but the resources that are included will point you in the right direction in your grant seeking efforts.

Grant Seeking

Contributions
PO Box 336
Medfield, MA 02052
508/359-0019
Cambridge Fund Raising Associates publishes this tabloid newspaper every other month. It emphasizes fundraising by providing practical tips, but is also helpful because it gives information on not-for-profit management, board development, and legal matters. It also publishes **Best of the Net**, a newsletter that updates web sites dealing with non-profit issues such as management and fund development.

Capitol Publications, Inc.
1101 King Street, PO Box 1453
Alexandria, VA 22313
703/683-4100
Federal Grants and Contracts Weekly is a weekly report on available federal grants and contracts. It includes a monthly supplement on

foundation funding, plus news analysis, updates of new legislation, regulations, publications, meetings, a calendar of deadlines, and more. Capitol publishes other newsletters that give similar information regarding health, education and people with disabilities. They also publish **The Grantseeker's Handbook of Internet Sites**.

CD Publications
8204 Fenton Street
Silver Spring, MD 20910
(800) 666-6380
This company publishes the **Federal Assistance Monitor** twice a month. It is a comprehensive review of federal funding announcements, private grants, rule changes and legislative actions affecting social services, arts, education, and health, plus advice on how to find funding and writing effective proposals.

The Center on Nonprofits and Philanthropy
2100 M Street, NW, Suite 500
Washington, DC 20037
202/857-8806
The Urban Institute, a nonprofit policy research organization established in Washington, DC, created The Center on Nonprofits and Philanthropy in 1996. Its purpose is to better understand nonprofits and philanthropy and to

strengthen and encourage the use of data that relates to these organizations. A component of the Center is the National Center For Charitable Statistics (NCCS). The mission of NCCS is to build compatible national, state, and regional databases and to develop uniform standards for reporting on activities of charitable organizations. Databases and reports from NCCS are available to researchers, nonprofits, government, businesses, and the public.

The Chronicle of Philanthropy
PO Box 1989
Marion, OH 43306
202/466-1200 (Editorial and business office)
Published every other week (except the last weeks of August and the last two weeks of December) by The Chronicle of Higher Education, Inc. this tabloid newspaper covers all the important aspects of nonprofit organizations and philanthropic activity. This is a necessary publication for anyone serious about learning and understanding the philanthropic world. It is the best and most thorough publication in the field. They also have a CD-ROM Guide to Grants, a database of over 30,000 grants awarded by over 1,500 funders.

Council on Foundations
1828 L Street, NW
Washington, DC 20036
202/466-6512

Council on Foundations publishes **Foundation News and Commentary** every other month. The Council is a national membership organization for grantmakers and this publication is their vehicle for communicating with one another. **Foundation News and Commentary** is written from a grantmaker's perspective, but grantseekers who read it will learn a great deal about soliciting grants from foundations.

The Foundation Center
79 Fifth Avenue
New York, NY 10003
800/424-9836
The Foundation Center is a national service organization established by foundations to disseminate information about philanthropic activities. The Center produces a number of reference materials, including **The Foundation Directory,** Part One and Two, **The Foundation 1000**, and **Foundation Grants Index**. They also produce a number of national guides and grant guides that are specific to various fields. The Center maintains a network of over 200 cooperating collections with public libraries, foundations, and support centers that aid grantseekers in researching foundations. The Center also has a CD-ROM data base of over 43,000 grantmakers and over 115,000 recent grants awarded. They distribute a quarterly catalog that describes their materials.

Government Information Service
1611 N. Kent Street Suite 508
Arlington, VA 22209
703/528-1000

Government Information Services(GIS) and its sibling, Education Funding Research Council (EFRC at the same address), both provide information relative to governmental agencies and education organizations regarding federal funding. Each year they produce a number of directories such as **Guide to Federal Funding for Education, Guide to Federal Funding for Anti-Drug Programs,** and **Guide to Federal Funding for Volunteer Programs.** Each group also markets a newsletter.

Institute for Educational Leadership
1001 Connecticut Ave. NW Suite 310
Washington, DC 20036
202/822-8405

The Institute for Educational Leadership is a nonpartisan organization that seeks to improve educational opportunities and results for children, youth and families by developing and supporting leaders who work together. Through a national publication program, it disseminates information about emerging trends and issues. The **CDP Demographics for Decision Makers Newsletter** is one of their publications. This quarterly newsletter identifies demographic trends that demonstrate the need for collaboration among diverse organizations in both the public and private sectors. Their other publications include **Bringing Tomorrow Into Focus: Demographic Insights for the Future**, **A Demographic Look At Tomorrow** and **Hispanic Americans: A Look Back, A Look Ahead**. They have also produced some state and regional demographic profiles.

National Center for Nonprofit Boards
2000 L Street NW, Suite 411
Washington, DC 20036
800/883-6262 or 202/452-6262
The Center is a membership organization that focuses on nonprofit organization boards of directors. It has a number of publications on effective boards and board governance. Members receive a 25 percent discount on publications. Additionally, the Center conducts a national conference and seminars. They distribute a quarterly catalog that describes their materials.

National Network of Grantmakers
1717 Kettner Boulevard
San Diego, CA 92101
619/231-1348
The National Network of Grantmakers is an organization that promotes a progressive agenda within philanthropic efforts. It consists of over 440 individual members and 28 institutional supporters, such as donors, trustees, board

members, and employees of grantmaking programs, and they work for systemic change to create social, political, economic, and environmental justice. They put out several publications, one of which is the Grantmakers Directory, which lists information on its members. They describe the publication as a reference tool and working document for NNG members, their funding programs, and progressive grantseekers.

Nonprofit Risk Management Center
1001 Connecticut Avenue, NW Suite 900
Washington, DC 20036
202/785-3891
The Nonprofit Risk Management Center helps community-serving nonprofits control risks so that they can achieve their missions. The Center provides a range of services, which include publications, training, and technical assistance. Two of their publications are particularly useful. One, **Crisis Management for Nonprofit Organizations: Ten Steps for Survival,** is an easy-to-read guide that will give staff and boards guidelines for reducing risks in their organizations. The other, **Healthy Nonprofits: Conserving Scarce Resources Through Effective Internal Controls**, provides in-depth information on maintaining and operating a healthy nonprofit corporation. Information includes how to reduce the danger of mismanagement, bad publicity, legal liability, and IRS scrutiny through risk management.

The NonProfit Times
190 Tamarack Circle
Skillman, NJ 08558
609/921-1251
Each issue contains news, features, interviews, plus articles on board development, foundations, and management. Sections included are News Briefs, Books, Calendar, Employment Marketplace, Newsmakers, and Directory. It is distributed without charge to "qualified full-time nonprofit executives who specify job title and responsibilities." To apply for a free subscription, write.

The Society For Nonprofit Organizations
6314 Odana Road, Suite 1
Madison, WI 53719
608/274-9774
The Society is a membership organization that offers various services to the nonprofit community, such as discounts on publications and travel. It publishes **Nonprofit World**, a magazine that provides articles on various subjects pertinent to nonprofit organizations, and **Nonprofit World Funding Alert**. Each month's edition of the **Funding Alert** provides an update of potential funding sources. This publication also profiles two foundations in each issue.

Superintendent of Documents
U.S. Government Printing Office
Washington, DC 20402

The United States Government publishes **The Catalog of Federal Domestic Assistance,** which contains more than 1000 pages of detailed information on federal domestic programs, including eligibility requirements, application procedures, and other pertinent information. This loose-leaf manual is published annually in May and is updated six months later. It is also available on CD-Rom and diskette. For information on these items you should contact the Federal Domestic Assistance Catalog Staff, General Services Administration, 300 7th St., SW, Washington, DC 20407. One other helpful publication available from the Superintendent's office is the **United States Government Manual**. This paperback describes every federal agency, department, commission, and quasi-government entity. It also lists addresses, telephone numbers, and key personnel for each. It makes a good companion for the Catalog.

The Taft Group
835 Penobscot Building
Detroit, MI 48226
800/877-8238
The Taft Group, a division of Gale Research, publishes a number of books, including **The Directory of Corporate and Foundation Givers**, **The Foundation Reporter**, and **Corporate Giving Directory**. Additionally they have several CD-ROMs, including **Grants on Disk**

that is a database of over 167,000 grants awarded by over 5,000 funders. They also have publications on non-grant fundraising and related subjects. They distribute a quarterly catalog that describes their materials.

The Grantsmanship Center
1125 W. Sixth Street, Fifth Floor
PO Box 17220
Los Angeles, CA 90017
213/482-9860
Since it was founded in 1972, the Center has trained over 72,000 people in program planning and proposal writing, program management, and fundraising. Training programs are conducted throughout the country, and four to six programs are offered during most weeks of the year. It also produces publications, including **Program Planning and Proposal Writing**, and offers insurance for nonprofit organizations. Its web site, http://www.tgci.com/, provides grant information that includes a summary of **Federal Register** grant announcements and a funding tip of the day. Additionally, the Center distributes a free magazine, **The Grantsmanship Center Magazine**, which is published on a somewhat quarterly basis.

Youth Today
1200 17th Street 4th floor
Washington, DC 20036
202/785-0764

The American Youth Work Center publishes **Youth Today**. It includes information on youth issues such as legislation, public policy and funding. This publication is useful for anyone even remotely involved with youth.

Publications

Boards

Board Overboard: Laughs and Lessons for All But the Perfect Nonprofits, Brian O'Connell, copyright 1996, Jossey-Bass Publishers, San Francisco, CA. ISBN 0-7879-0179-2

Boards That Make A Difference: A New Design for Leadership in Nonprofit and Public Organizations, John Carver, Jossey-Bass Publishers, San Francisco, California, ISBN 1-55542-231-4

Boardroom Verities, Jerold Panas, copyright 1991, Precept Press, Inc., Chicago, IL. ISBN 0-944496-26-1

Governing Boards: Their Nature and Nurture, Cyril O. Houle, Jossey-Bass Publishers, San Francisco, CA. ISBN 1-55542-157-1

10 Minutes to Better Board Meetings, Norah Holmgren, copyright 1994, Planned Parenthood

Federation of America Western Region Office, 333 Broadway, 3rd floor, San Francisco, CA 94133.

The Board Member's Book: Making a Difference in Voluntary Organizations, 2nd edition, Brian O'Connell, copyright 1993, The Foundation Center, New York, NY. ISBN 0-87954-502-X

Fundraising

Building a Strong Foundation: Fundraising for Nonprofits, Richard L. Edwards and Elizabeth A. S. Benefield with Jeffrey A. Edwards and John A. Yankey, copyright 1997, NASW Press National Association of Social Workers, 750 First Street, NE Washington, DC 20002. ISBN 0-87101-249-9

Discover Total Resources: A Guide for Nonprofits, copyright 1995, Mellon Bank Corporation, One Mellon Bank Center, Community Affairs Division, Pittsburgh, PA.

How the Denver Children's Museum Earns $600,000 Annually: Nonprofit Piggy Goes To Market, Children's Museum of Denver, Inc., copyright 1984, 2121 Crescent Drive, Denver, CO 80211

Raising Money, Having Fun (sort of) A "How To" Book for Small Non-Profit Groups, Charlene Horton, Mary Dugan Center, 4115 Bridge Avenue, Cleveland, OH. 44113. ISBN 0-9630760-0-0

Internet

The Grantseeker's Handbook of Essential Internet Sites, Second Edition, James DeAngelis, Editor, 1997, Capitol Publications, Inc., Alexandria, VA, ISBN 1-56925-096-0

The Nonprofit Guide to the Internet, Robin Zeff, copyright, John Wiley & Son, Inc., New York, NY. ISBN 0-471-15359-1

Where the Information Is: A Guide to Electronic Research for Nonprofit Organizations, Helen Bergan, copyright 1996, BioGuide Press

Not-For-Profit Legal

Nonprofit Corporations, Organizations, and Associations, Fifth Edition, Howard L. Oleck, copyright 1994, Prentice Hall, Inc., NJ. ISBN 0-13-623363-5

Reconsidering Legal Liability and Insurance For Organizations, Charles Robert Tremper, copyright 1989, The Society for Nonprofit Organizations, Madison, WI. ISBN 0-9622304-0-5

Not-for-Profit Marketing

How to Tell and Sell Your Story: A Guide to Media for Community Groups and Other Nonprofits, Issue 18, Winter 1997, Center for Community Change, 1000 Wisconsin, Washington, DC 20007.

Marketing Workbook for Nonprofit Organizations, Gary J. Stern, copyright 1990, Amherst H. Wilder Foundation, St. Paul, MN. ISBN 0-940-06901-6

Not-for-Profit Management

A Nonprofit Organization Operating Manual, Arnold J. Olenick and Philip R. Olenick, Copyright 1991, The Foundation Center, New York, NY. ISBN 0-87954-293-4

Managing A Nonprofit Organization, Thomas Wolf, copyright 1991, Prentice Hall Press, New York, NY. ISBN 0-13-551557-2

Potpourri

The Fifth Discipline, Peter M. Senge, copyright 1990, Currency Doubleday, New York. ISBN 0-385-26095-4

Future Edge, Joel Arthur Barker, copyright 1992, William Morrow and Company, New York. ISBN 0-688-10936-51

The New Doublespeak, William Lutz, copyright 1996, Harpers Collins Publishers, New York ISBN 0-06-017134-0

Politics

Politics For Dummies®, Ann Delaney, copyright 1995, IDG Books Worldwide, Inc. Foster City, CA. ISBN 1-56884-381-X

Proposal Writing

The Foundation Center's Guide to Proposal Writing, New Revised Edition, Jane C. Geever, Patricia McNeill, copyright 1997, The Foundation Center. ISBN 0-87954-703-0

Grassroots Grants: An Activist's Guide to Proposal Writing, Andy Robinson, copyrights 1996, Chardon Press, PO Box 11607, Berkeley, CA 94712. ISBN 0-9620222-5-X

Research

**American Library Association Guide to Information Access: A Complete Research

Handbook and Directory, Sandy Whiteley, Editor, copyright 1994, Random House, New York, ISBN 0-0679-43060-1

Writing

A Writer's Reference, Third Edition, Diana Hacker, copyright 1995, Bedford Books of St. Martin's Press, Boston, MA. ISBN 0-312-13417-7

Line by Line: How To Improve Your Own Writing, copyright 1985, Claire Kehrwald Cook, Houghton Mifflin Company, Boston, MA. ISBN 0-395-39391-4

Make Your Words Work, Gary Provost, copyright 1990, Writer's Digest Books, Cincinnati, OH. ISBN 0-89879-636-9

Simple & Direct: A Rhetoric for Writers, Revised Edition, Jacques Barzun, copyright 1985, The University of Chicago Press, Chicago, IL. ISBN 0-226-03868-8

The Bias-Free Word Finder: A Dictionary of Nondiscriminatory Language, copyright 1991, Rosalie Maggio, Beacon Press, Boston, MA. ISBN 0-8070-6003-8

The Elements of Style, Third Edition, copyright 1979, Strunk, William, Jr. and White, E.B., Macmillan Publishing Co., New York, NY.

Type & Layout, Colin Wheildon, copyright 1995, Strathmoor Press Inc., Berkeley, CA. ISBN 0-9624891-5-8

Write Tight: How to Keep Your Prose Sharp, Focused and Concise, William Brohaugh, copyright 1993, Writer's Digest Books, Cincinnati, OH. ISBN 0-89879-548-6

Writing With Precision, Jefferson D. Bates, copyright 1994, Acropolis South, L.C., Sarasota, FL. ISBN 0-87491-991-6

Special Interest Funding Guides

Environmental Data Research Institute
P.O. Box 22770
Rochester, NY 14692-2770

Publishes **The Environmental Grantmaking Foundations**, which gives in-depth information on a broad cross-section of environmental grantmakers.

Resource Women
4527 South Dakota Ave., NE
Washington, DC 20017

Publishes **Religious Funding Resource Guide**. This guide covers religious funding and includes Ecumenical, Episcopal, Jewish, Lutheran, Presbyterian, Catholic, Unitarian, Methodist, and United Church of Christ funders.

About the Author

VC League works with Vincente` & Associates, a consulting and training group located in Oakland, California. For nine years he was president of a not-for-profit corporation that was based in Oakland and had offices and projects in five cities. He has consulted with over 1900 organizations throughout the United States, Canada, the Bahamas, and all U.S. territories. This work has included program planning and proposal writing, coalition building, and organization and board development. He has served on over 25 boards of directors and is currently the secretary-treasurer of Prevention Partnership, Inc., located in Chicago. VC has written over 50 articles for publications ranging from newsletters to national magazines. He is also co-author of ***Developing Successful Programs*** and ***Prevention Funding: A Resource Guide for Grant Development.***

++++

VC League is available to answer questions regarding program planning, proposal writing, or researching funding sources. He can be reached by e-mail at TVLVC@aol.com or at 510/446-7736.

++++

Curry-Co Publications is not responsible for the delivery or content of the information or materials provided by the author. The reader should address any questions to the author at the above numbers or Vincente` & Associates, 2101 Webster Street, Suite 1500, Oakland, CA 94612.

References

First Thoughts

Chin-Ning Chu, *Thick Face, Black Heart*, (New York: Warner Books, 1992)

Changing Times

"War on Nonprofits Heats Up," *Nonprofit World*, Vol. 14, No. 1, 1986, Madison, WI

Tom Peters, *The Tom Peters Seminar: Crazy Times Call for Crazy Organizations*, (New York: Vintage Book, 1994)

The Seven Laws of Money

Michael Phillips, *The Seven Laws of Money*, (Menlo Park, CA: Word Wheel and Random House, 1974)

Joseph Campbell, *The Power of Myth*, (New York: Doubleday, 1988)

How to Say It!

William Strunk, Jr., and E.B. White, *The Elements of Style*, (New York: Macmillan Publishing Co., Inc, 1979)

Haig A. Bosmajian, *The Language of Oppression*, (University Press of America, 1983)

William Lutz, *The New Doublespeak*, (New York: Harpers Collins Publishers, 1996)

Rosalie Maggio, *The Bias-Free Word Finder*, (Boston: Beacon Press, 1991)

Program Planning

Joel Arthur Barker, *Future Edge*, (New York: William Morrow And Company, 1992)

"United Way Cuts Stun Community," *Oakland Tribune* (CA), May 17, 1996

Kirsten A. Gronbjerg, *Understanding Nonprofit Funding: Managing Revenues in Social Services and Community Development Organizations*, (San Francisco: Jossey-Bass, 1993)

VC League, *Developing Successful Programs*, (Oakland, CA: AHTDS Publications, Fourth Edition, 1986)

VC League, *Independent Contractor or Employee*, Paper Published by Vincente` Publications, Decatur, GA, 1993

Norton J. Kiritz, *Program Planning and Proposal Writing*, (Los Angeles: The Grantsmanship Center, 1980)

Virginia A. Lathan, VC League, Ann F. Monroe, *Prevention Funding: A Resource Guide for Grant Development* (Springfield, IL: Project PRC, 1981)

Andy Robinson, *Grassroots Grants: An Activist's Guide to Proposal Writing*, (Berkeley, CA: Chardon Press, 1996)

Ed Sanchez, *Diversity and Prevention*, (unpublished paper, 1993)

Peter M. Senge, *The Fifth Discipline*, (New York: Currency Doubleday, 1990)

Karen Sue Trisko and VC League, "Evaluation of Human-Service Programs," *The 1980 Annual Handbook for Group Facilitators,* University Associates, San Diego, CA, Chapter 10

Who Are These People?

Norton J. Kiritz, *Program Planning and Proposal Writing*, (Los Angeles, CA: The Grantsmanship Center, 1980)

Just Where is the Money?

Warren Bennis and Patricia Ward Biedeman, *Organizing Genius: The Secrets of Creative*

Collaboration, (Reading, MA, Addison-Wesley Publishing Company, Inc. 1997

Stalking the Elusive Dollars in Cyberspace

Roy Tennant, John Ober, Anne G. Lipow, *Crossing the Internet Threshold*, (Berkeley, CA: Library Solutions Press, 1993

Robin Zeff, *The Nonprofit Guide to the Internet*, (New York: John Wiley & Son, 1996)

"Da Board"

Peter F. Drucker, *Managing The Nonprofit Organization,* (New York: Harper Collins Publishers, 1990)

Thomas Wolf, *Managing a Nonprofit Organization*, (New York: Prentice Hall Press, 1990)

VC's Recommended Resources

Boise Public Library, for assistance provided by Mary K. Jones Aucutt, Funding Information Center, Boise Public Library Boise, Idaho.

Index

501(c)(3), 106, 110, 158
60 Minutes, 168
Abrams, Peter 11
Advocacy, 3-5, 117
Amendment, 5, 6
American Association of Retired Persons, 4
America On Line (AOL), 137-138
Angelou, Maya, 21
Applicant agency (as relates to credibility), 101, 108
Associated Press Style Book and Libel Manual, 22
Aucutt, Mary K. Jones, 172
Babas, 17
Barker, Joel Arthur, 2
Bell South Foundation, 145
Bennis, Warren, 114
Bias Free Word Finder, 42
Biedeman, Patricia Ward, 114
Board Members, 6
Board of directors (as relates to fundraising), 151-166
Boise Idaho Public Library, 172
Bosmajian, Haig, 40
Browsers, 136
Budget (explored), 88-96
Bulletin boards, 137, 145
California, 11, 46, 85, 134-135, 146, 148
Campbell, Joseph, 20
Capra, Fritjof, 55
Catalog of Federal Domestic Assistance, 127, 129, 146
Center for Substance Abuse Prevention, 83, 146
Charles A. Dana, 145
Chicago Manual of Style, 23
Chronicle of Philanthropy, 117, 129
Chu, Chin-Ning, 11-12
Clinton, 32, 135
Colorado Association of Nonprofits, 6
Community networks, 138
CompuServe, 138
Congress, 4, 6, 10, 84

Council of Foundations, 146
Credibility gaps, 102
Crossing the Internet Threshold, 148
Curtis, Jody 146
Dateline NBC, 168
Department of Labor, 91
Developing Successful Programs, 47
Dialog, 139
Diversity and Prevention, 49
Donor groups, 118
Doublespeak, 28 30-31
Dow Jones, 139
Drucker, Peter F., 151
Dynamic flow, 18
Easter Seal, 41
Ehrlich, Robert L., 5
Einstein, Albert, 51
Electronic databases, 139
Elements of Style, 23, 26
E-mail, 136-139
English teacher test, 27
Fair use, 37
Federal Assistance Monitor, 129
Federal Grants and Contracts Weekly, 129
Federal Register, 128, 146
Fifth Discipline, 55
Fifth Law, 18
First Amendment, 5
First Law, 13
Foundation 1000, 116
Foundation Center, 116-117, 139, 146, 169
Foundation Center Grant Guides, 116
Foundation News and Commentary, 146
Foundation Reporter, 142
Fourth Law, 16
Freirian Stance, 49-50
Future Edge, 2
Global Fund for Women, 87
Gore, 135
Grammar hotline(s), 28

Index 199

Grantsmanship Center, 13, 34, 47, 101, 106, 109, 128, 143, 146
Grant Guide for Minorities, 116
Grant Guide, 116
Grantseeker's Handbook of Essential Internet Sites, 142, 150
Grant Seekers Guide, 117
Gronbjerg, Kristen A., 79
Guide for Minorities, 116
Guillery, Joanne, 51
Hacker, Diana, 23
HandsNet, 138
Home page, 140, 144
I Know Why the Caged Bird Sings, 21
Independent contractor (IRS criteria), 77, 91-95
Indiana Donor Alliance, 118
Indiana Prevention Resource Center, 145
In Search of Excellence, 1
Internal Revenue Service (IRS), 93, 95, 106
Internet service providers, 138-140, 144
Internet, 124, 130, 132-137-139, 141-150, 168, 172
Introduction (to proposal), 101
Istook, Ernest J., 5
Jackson, Bailey 16
Lamb, David, 142
Language of Oppression, 40
Lathan, Virginia, 51
Lexis/Nexus, 139
Lutz, William, 29, 30
Lynch, Clifford, 148-150
Maggio, Rosalie, 42
Managing a Nonprofit Organization, 154, 165
Managing the Nonprofit Organization, 152
Martin, Edna, 14, 159
McIntosh, David M., 5
Mega Trends, 124
Methods (explored), 60-61
Michigan Council of Foundations, 118
Microsoft Network (MSN), 137
Model programs, 66, 145
Murray, Anne Firth, 87
Naming the population, 40

Nasbitt, John, 124
National Council for Nonprofit Associations, 6
National Network of Grantmakers, 117
Needs statement (explored), 55-56
Needs Assessment: A Manual for Community Action, 51
Net (Internet) 133-134, 136, 138, 140-141, 147
NetDay '96, 135
New York Public Library Writer's Guide of Style and Usage, 23
New Doublespeak: Why No One Knows What Anyone's Saying Anymore, 28
Non-discriminatory language, 37-39
Non-sexist language, 37-39
Nonprofit Guide to the Internet, 133
Now What? (explained), 16, 167
Organization capability (as relates to credibility), 104
Organization credibility, 106-108, 157
Organizing Genius: The Secrets of Creative Collaboration, 114
Outcome evaluations, 61, 71, 74
Paradigm Shift, 2
Pedagogy of the Oppressed, 49
People First Rule, 42
Peters, Tom, 1-2
Phillips, Michael, 11, 14-15, 18, 20
Philosophy of fund development, 159-161
President, 135
Prevline, 145
Prevnet, 145
Problem statement (explored), 51-53
Program Planning and Proposal Writing (The Grantsmanship Center Publication), 47, 106
Program objectives (explored), 57-60
    Five Criteria for, 57-58
    Exercise, 98-100
Proposal summary (explored), 96-97
Readiness plan (contents of), 110
Robinson, Andy, 87
Rutgers University, 28
Sackey, Ann Mitchell, 6

SAMHSA, 83-84
Sanchez, Ed, 49, 147
San Francisco, 11, 21, 84-85
Second Law, 14
Senate, 4
Senge, Peter, 55
Services and Community Development
 Organizations, 79
Sexist language, 37-39
So What? (explained), 16
Spanish (learning to speak), 46-47
State directories of foundations, 117
Strunk, William, Jr., 23, 26
Substance Abuse and Mental Health
 Services Administration, 83
Substance Abuse Funding News, 129
Swahili, 17
Systems approach, 54
Systems thinking 54
 Senge's caveats for becoming a better, 55-56
Texas Center for Nonprofit Resources, 118
Thick Face, Black Heart, 11
Third Law, 15
Tom Peters Seminar: Crazy Times Call for
 Crazy Organizations 1
Understanding Nonprofit Funding
 and Managing Revenue in Social Services
 and Community Development Organizations, 79
Uniform resource locator (UR:), 139
United States Government Manual, 128
United Way, 10, 17, 84-86, 89
Unrestricted funds, 161-162
U.S. Department of Justice, 16
VC, 41
Vincente` & Associates, 13
Waterman, Jr., Robert H., 1
Weber, Max, 42

Webster's New World Dictionary, 102
Web site (defined), 139
What? (explained), 16
White, E.B. 23, 26
Wilson, Gaddy, 42
Wolf, Thomas, 154-155
    Six Areas of Responsibility for Boards of Directors, 165
Working With Words, 42
World Wide Web, 134, 135, 138, 139, 144
Zeff, Robin, 133

Order Form for Curry-Co Publications

P.O. Box 231097 - Sacramento, CA 95823-1097
Phone/Fax 916/395-1133
E-mail curryco@softcom.net
Web Site http://www.curry-co-pub.com

Quantity./Cost

The Proposal Writer's Workshop:
A Guide to Help You Write Winning
Proposals; by VC League;
trade paperback; 195 pgs. $24.95   _____

Developing Successful Programs;
by VC League; Steve Oliver and
Karen Trisko; soft cover;
spiral bound; 63 pgs $6.95   _____

Needs Assessment; A Manual for
Community Action; by Joanne Guillery
and Virginia Lathan;
soft cover; spiral bound; 72 pgs $7.95   _____

California Add 7.75% Sales Tax   _____
Shipping & Handling $4.00
   Add $1.00 for each book over 1   _____
                            TOTAL $_____

(Check One)
Check Encl. _____   Money Ord. Encl. _____
(Circle One)
VISA , MasterCard, AmExp., or Purchase Order

Number_____
Expiration Date on Credit Card_____

Print Name on Card_____

Signature_____
Telephone No._____

- Over -

Ship To_____

_____
_____
_____
_____

Books are usually shipped within 48 hrs. by UPS or USPS. Call if other shipping arrangements desired.
Mail to Curry-Co Publications, P.O. Box 231097, Sacto. 95823-1097; or Fax to: 916/395-1133